FREEDOM
TO DREAM
COURAGE
TO ACT

bright sky press
HOUSTON, TEXAS

bright sky press
HOUSTON, TEXAS

2365 Rice Blvd., Suite 202
Houston, Texas 77005

ISBN: 978-1-939055-84-2

10 9 8 7 6 5 4 3 2 1

Library of Congress Cataloging-in-Publication Data on file with publisher.

Editorial Direction, Lucy Herring Chambers
Editor, Eva Freeburn
Design, Marla Y. Garcia

Printed in Canada through Friesens

FREEDOM

TO DREAM

COURAGE

TO ACT

The First Nine Decades of C. Jackson Grayson

JOHN DeMERS *AND* PAIGE DAWSON

"What a marvelously wonderful life! Jack's book was as much an inspiration upon reading as knowing him for over twenty years and living within his dream, while watching him stimulate others to action. As one who has been stimulated to act by Jack, I can vouch that his dreaming is contagious and creates in others the desire to be a better human being. Thank you for being Jack Grayson!"

— **GREGORY H. WATSON**
Past Chairman, American Society for Quality
Past Chairman, International Academy for Quality

"*Freedom to Dream, Courage to Act: The First Nine Decades of C. Jackson Grayson* offers a fascinating insight into one of the most creative people I have ever known. Having worked closely with Jack Grayson from 1968-1975 and observed his relentless pursuit to change our country through improvements in our education system and our economy, I have no doubt that he will long be remembered as one of the outstanding thought leaders of our time. Never content with the status quo, this academic gypsy, entrepreneur, author, public servant and patriot has pushed the boundaries of creative thought and action at every stage of his professional career. Every organization with which he has worked and the people within those organizations are better for his having passed their way. I was one of those whose life was changed forever as a result of knowing and working with Jack. This biography provides a glimpse at this remarkable man, his dreams and his journey. As he has always been fond of saying: 'Things don't just happen; someone has to make it happen.' For the first 90 years of his life…Jack did! And, he's still going strong! I can't wait for the next chapter!"

— **BOBBY B. LYLE**
Founder
Lyco Holdings Incorporated

"Jack Grayson is the epitome of life-long learning. Over the years I have been collaborating with Jack, I had heard snippets of many of his learning experiences described in the book. It was a real delight to get the 'full story' in the biography. Jack Grayson has made and continues to make significant contributions in business, education and other fields. *Freedom to Dream, Courage to Act* provides a shining example of how to lead a full and rewarding life, and I highly recommend the book as an excellent read to gain insights for excellent leadership and life skills."

> – **TERRY HOLLIDAY, Ph.D.**
> *Commissioner of Education*
> *Commonwealth of Kentucky*

"Having known Jack Grayson for over 40 years, I never cease to be amazed by his knowledge, his productivity, enthusiasm and desire to change the business world. I am convinced that much of this has been accomplished by his dedication to his personal health and fitness programs. He is one of the few people I have known who have actually 'grown healthier as they have grown older, and not the reverse.'"

> – **KENNETH H. COOPER, M.D., M.P.H.**
> *Founder and Chairman*
> *Cooper Aerobics Center, Dallas, Texas*

"In this age of discussing why you CAN'T do something, it is delightful to follow the life and multiple careers of a person who seeks out problems and gets them solved. In founding and growing APQC, Jack led his employees to the ideas and authority to make the needed difference, but we always knew in reaching out for the innovative (and perhaps riskier) solution, Jack would be there at crunch time with more ideas. Let's hope for the sake of the country that his recent education initiative turns out to be his most successful of all."

> – **CARL G. THOR**
> *Owner/Artist, JarrettThor Fine Arts*
> *Former President and Director of Measurement, APQC*
> *Member, Board of Directors, APQC*

"Jack Grayson is a truly great American icon whose love of country and his fellow man drives his innovative and restless spirit to constantly strive to improve the human condition not only in the United States but throughout the world. To Jack Grayson, the greatest gift this country has given both the world and him is the freedom to dream and act to achieve personal dreams. With that twinkle in his eye and smile on his face, Jack has given that same gift to so many, for so many years and through his own actions inspired them to have the courage to succeed. Knowing Jack personally, working with him, learning from him, being inspired by him and being able to refer to him as a friend and colleague, is a gift that I will cherish forever. The book is an extraordinary treatise about one of the truly great individuals of our time who helped shape the annals of history by teaching others to embrace the *Freedom to Dream* and the *Courage to Act.*"

> **– MICHAEL P. PERICH**
> *Friend and Colleague*
> *Systemwide Coordinator Continuous Improvement*
> *Montgomery County Public Schools*

"Few individuals have accomplished more, or been as effective, in changing the direction of the free enterprise system in fundamental and lasting ways than Jack Grayson. Certainly no one has more dramatically raised the level of awareness of productivity and quality or restored American businesses and education better. I have been fortunate to share part of this remarkable journey with him and experience his magic and ability to unleash the entrepreneurial spirit in others."

> **– LISA HIGGINS**
> *President and COO*
> *APQC*

"To meet Jack Grayson once is to be inspired by his optimism, vision and energy. This tale of a remarkable life will inspire anyone to dream. But more importantly to dare... You only have to meet Jack Grayson once to know he's a remarkable man. He fills a room with new possibilities and the courage to dream. I can only wonder what new mountain Jack will climb next. If ever you feel this world holds no new expeditions, read this book. Jack forged new paths against much more formidable obstacles than lack of oxygen. And delightfully he took many of us along those journeys. Jack Grayson is one of America's great orchestrators. A man of vision, surely, but a man with the ability to inspire others to join doubtful journeys too crucial to leave unexplored. Jack Grayson's life is a gift and gives us all good reason to dream, to gather courage and be grateful for our freedom to act. This account of his life makes that gift available to anyone who needs inspiration to embark on a journey against the odds. A delightfully inspiring life...of challenge against great odds and of vision, risk, determination and reward."

 – PAUL E. BORAWSKI
 CEO (Retired)
 American Society for Quality

"John DeMers and Paige Dawson's biography of C. Jackson Grayson is a fascinating read. The authors render a very honest, objective story of the first nine decades of Jack Grayson's amazing life. It is a wonderful portrayal inclusive of Jack's feelings, beliefs, behavior and rationale for his actions relative to the particular time period. The details of his diverse life coupled with the obvious strength of his character will capture and hold the interest of any reader. Despite the incredible variety of Jack's experiences, a unifying theme pervades the book. Jack Grayson is a pioneer driven by dreams which he couples with determination, persistence, ingenuity and action. This book delivers his visions and the steps he has taken to make them reality. The wisdom imparted from this biography will empower anyone's life. As Jack says, 'enough of the past; your journey begins now.'"

 – BRADLEY F. BALE, M.D.
 Medical Director, Heart Health Program
 Grace Clinic

"For more than three decades now I've been privileged to join the adventure and witness the energy and spirit that is Jack Grayson, both professionally and personally. At 90, Jack is still out to change the world and having a blast doing it, as for him there is no distinction between work and play—it's all play. Before I met him, I had only read about people like Jack. Mischievous and fearless—even skydiving at age 90 his blood pressure didn't rise—smart, tireless and driven, Jack is a force of nature (a natural phenomenon if you will) out to transform the way we work and learn. And, as you'll see, he has done and continues to break new ground for individuals, business, government, education and nonprofit entities. He never gives up, never accepts the word 'no' and never thinks 'inside the box.' While it's hard to believe that one man could achieve so much and make such an impact on how we think, manage and invent the future, Jack (aka Mr. Charisma) will inspire you to do the same. While this book focuses chiefly on his zest for business aspects, he exhibits equal energy in pursuits for family, travel, health and laughter. Life with Jack has been a heck of a ride—sweet and exciting always, scary sometimes, boring never."

– **CARLA O'DELL**
CEO, APQC
and Wife of Jack Grayson

PREFACE

I FIND MYSELF EMPATHETIC TO MICHEL DE Montaigne, who wrote his autobiography about 400 years ago in Bordeaux, France. He had studied law and served for thirteen years as a magistrate in the Bordeaux parliament. But he became tired of intrigues of law and politics and retired to his medieval chateau to answer the age-old riddles *Who am I? What do I know? What should I do?* He considered himself an "unpremeditated philosopher," writing continuously for many years and producing a tome of 1200 pages. He wrote near the end of it: "I hope death finds me still planting cabbages."

In one important way we are alike. His philosophy was that a person can master events by mastering his or her attitude toward them. Amen. Yet in many other ways we differ. First, I don't like cabbages. Second, I choose not to retire and write an autobiography, but to never retire and to invite others (John DeMers and Paige Dawson) to ask the same questions. Based on what they see, and hear, I want them to give me *their* answer to these questions. I'm looking forward to reading what they have to say.

In the meantime, I'm not going to stop planting and implementing ideas. Right now, I'm planning to transform the entire US public education system. Over to you, John and Paige. And please—not 1200 pages!

Jack

TABLE OF CONTENTS

INTRODUCTION

IN CELEBRATING HIS NINETIETH BIRTHDAY, Dr. Charles Jackson "Jack" Grayson looks to his great-great-great-uncle for a certain kind of inspiration.

Hailing from a tiny rural bend in a north Louisiana road called Fort Necessity, Andrew Jackson Grayson must have taken his name seriously, compiling a list of risk-taking firsts that rivals those of his namesake, the great American hero and president. This Grayson traveled beyond the limits of nineteenth century civilization in the 1840s, west to California and south into Mexico, painting birds and other wildlife that Americans along the East Coast had never seen before. These works can still be viewed today at the University of California, Berkeley, the artistic legacy of a man widely admired as "The Audubon of the West."

Through important periods of his life, Andrew Jackson Grayson organized wagon trains that left barely-tamed outposts like St. Louis to cross uncharted expanses on the way to California. At one point, with winter coming on, Grayson chose a southern route to the Pacific, survived the hard journey and prospered buying real estate in San Francisco, while another group chose to head north and cross the snowy Sierra mountain passes in hopes of a shortcut. Tragically, few members of the northern group, the Donner party, survived to enjoy the rewards of their perseverance and sacrifice.

Today, at an age when most people are devoted to golf or even

less active retirements, Jack Grayson works to follow in his ancestor's footsteps. He goes into the office every day to show Americans (and others around an increasingly connected world) things they've never seen before. He still tries, especially in terms of business productivity, to help people, metaphorically, to prosper in Gold Rush San Francisco rather than perish in the snowy Sierras. Given the daunting unknowns facing American business in the twenty-first century, he is still very much organizing wagon trains across uncharted territory.

Jack believes in freedom, but not the kind that's easy, cheap, empty or entitled. As he is a three-year Navy veteran of the South Pacific during World War II, really, how could it be? In fact, if you listen long enough, you realize he uses the words "freedom" and "dream" frequently—sometimes in the same sentence—and a profound relationship between them is implied. To Jack Grayson, the greatest gift this country has given both the world and him is the freedom to dream and act to achieve personal dreams. When such freedom is allowed to flourish, Jack believes, there is no challenge too difficult to overcome, no adversary too powerful to confront. Dreaming and acting toward a better time, a better way and a better world is what freedom empowers. To Jack, it's what freedom *does*.

For anyone who figures a man with so much success in business would have to be serious, a man with so much success in government would have to be somber and a man with so much success in academia would have to be boring, meeting Jack Grayson is a shock. He seems, at any moment, both tremendously alive and irresistibly playful, giving himself over to quiet laughter at any good story—whether his own, a longtime friend's or a complete stranger's. Though he did once hand down his own set of laws, Jack seems less excited when he gets to tell someone a Great Truth than when that person suddenly verbalizes it. Only then does Jack nod gently, the ultimate satisfied smile spreading across his face. He sees himself as a lifelong teacher, which means that the only thing he really has to wake up and do each day is *learn*.

After earning a bachelor's degree from Tulane University, a

master's from the Wharton School of Business at the University of Pennsylvania and a doctorate from Harvard Business School, and after serving as a professor on four esteemed campuses and business dean on two of them, Jack has read more than his share of books. But what's most striking is how little of what he knows seems academic, literary or the least bit second-hand. Beginning on the same hard-scrabble north Louisiana farm that gave the world his great-great-great-uncle, Jack has pulled together a resume that's as quirky as it is long. How many certified public accountants, for instance, spent time as a reporter for a daily newspaper? How many newspaper reporters spent time as an FBI agent? Or as an importer-exporter? Or as a private pilot? And really, how many veterans of such diverse endeavors find themselves on the boards of multinational corporations or appointed to the Cabinet by the President of the United States?

Many who know Jack would agree that his wisdom comes not only from the many things he knows but also from the many things he's done. The latter shapes the former, it seems, and opens the door to no small number of highly entertaining yarns.

Take, for instance, the time when Jack was a young reporter for the *Item* in New Orleans. He wrote his first-ever news story about a murder and his editor kept sending it back, demanding a shorter and shorter lede, or opening sentence. Becoming frustrated, even though he'd never written a single word for a newspaper before, Jack decided to give his editor precisely that: a single word. "Dead," the cub reporter pecked out, then hit the typewriter's carriage return to add a short second paragraph: "That's what the man was when the police found him."

Or the time George Shultz, who served as President Nixon's Secretary of State and played many other roles in the White House, asked Jack to be the nation's only director of price controls, a job he'd later describe in a book as "an eclectic mixture of economics, power, pressure and politics." Once Jack heard the job description he replied, "But I don't *believe* in price controls." A shrewd judge of both people and politics, Shultz thought for a moment and then

smiled. "Exactly," he said. "That's why I want you to run them."

Jack's work in terms of business innovations, methodologies, awards and recognition has been well-documented over the decades. In 1990, *Business Week* said of him, "Few, if any, individual Americans have done more during the last 20 years to shape the country's economic future for the better." The same could be said for the twenty-plus years that have followed the article.

"The journey begins where you are," Jack often tells visitors to his own egalitarian, low-walled cubicle among six-dozen others at the American Productivity & Quality Center (APQC) in Houston, a nonprofit benchmarking, best practices and knowledge management organization he founded shortly after his White House experience. Speaking these words, Jack aspires to sound hopeful, reassuring— even when the guidance he ends up giving to companies, cities, states, nations and, increasingly, education systems, may seem traumatic, verging on the surgical. That's because Jack actually *is* hopeful, actually *is* reassuring. He believes in the ability of human beings, individually but particularly working as a team (thus the low walls at APQC) to get very large things done in real time.

To know and understand Jack Grayson, however, it isn't enough to begin where *he* is now, as pleasant a pastime as that may be. You have to peel away nearly nine decades of living and working, moving back into an earlier century and, to include Andrew Jackson Grayson, perhaps the century before that. You have to journey backwards, slipping past people who are no more and places that are no longer the same. You have to start at the beginning.

UNCLE JACK

CHARLES JACKSON GRAYSON BEGAN HIS voyage of discovery in the fertile, dark-soiled delta created by the Mississippi River when he learned of an ancestor with a name strikingly similar to his own: Andrew Jackson "A.J." Grayson. As a child known as "Charlie Jack," thanks to that Deep South proclivity for double names, Charlie Jack heard one of his cousins speak of "Uncle Jack." That conversation would make all the difference in Jack's life.

"My cousin was always poking around things," Jack says. Most people he encountered during his childhood let things be just as they always had been. They didn't go stirring up the past or looking to the future. Once the cousin started "poking around," though, what emerged into the lives of Jack and his family was little short of amazing.

Jack comes by risk taking naturally. To get a glimpse into the entrepreneurial and adventurous spirit of the Grayson family over the generations, we first step back to the 1800s to set the stage.

Andrew Jackson Grayson had grown up on this same land, but he had been sent north to St. Louis after trouble at school. He had organized wagon trains west, had made it to California a couple of years before the Gold Rush and had amassed considerable wealth in merchandising and real estate. He had studied western birds and other wildlife for the Smithsonian Institution. And perhaps most impressive of all, he had painted what he called "Birds of the Pacific Slope" with so much beauty and scientific detail that he came to be respected by the nation's naturalists as the "Audubon of the West." There were fortunes made and fortunes lost, all against the freewheeling backdrop of a dazzlingly beautiful country with more energy than rules.

Late in his life, A.J. had done the same thing Charlie Jack would come to do whenever he experienced something memorable or important. He set pen to paper and told the whole story. Today, A.J. Grayson's autobiography is a remarkable family document. After at least two generations of neglect—paralleling the time A.J.'s bird paintings rested in obscurity in Berkeley—Jack became fascinated by his relative. Like the rest of his family, Charlie Jack came to admire and even love his late relative. He found in his ancestor a hero worthy of emulation in more ways than he could count.

The Grayson family, with roots in both England and Ireland, came to Louisiana by way of Kentucky. They settled in a place that still clung to its cultural roots in France and Spain, that still measured land in old deeds in French *arpents* rather than American acres and that still did business and passed down property by the exotic principles of the Napoleonic Code. The Louisiana Purchase had occurred only fifteen years before A.J.'s birth as the twelfth of Thomas and Sarah Grayson's thirteen children.

The Graysons acquired a small piece of land in an area known as Bouef (Beef) Prairie, following the still practiced local custom of simplifying the French to sound like "Beff." An early explorer had sighted some American bison in the vicinity, so the area and the river that ran through it from the Mississippi got its name. There were no real businesses except for those miles away by mule, no churches and no

schools—until A.J. neared his tenth birthday and the community con-
structed a school. Soon after, an Irishman named Tobin arrived. His
tenure at the school, being given living quarters on the Grayson prop-
erty, is one of the first memorable set-pieces in A.J.'s autobiography.

"It was during this time that I made my first attempts at drawing,
taking sly moments when old Tobin was having his noonday snooze
in his armchair. I was engaged one day upon my last picture which
I called a river scene, with a canoe in the river and two Choctaw
Indians paddling it. Old Tobin had waked up and seeing two boys
peeking over my shoulders watching the progress of the picture, he
slyly came up and caught me in the act," he wrote.

A.J. was in trouble, clearly, for creating art on a slate rather than
working in his lessons. Enraged, Tobin demanded the boy pull out
all the art that resided in his desk and, when he refused, dealt him a
"severe blow on the side of the head." A.J. responded by picking up
his slate and smashing it over Tobin's head.

That evening, Tobin angrily showed all A.J.'s drawings to his fa-
ther, complaining about how much valuable time the boy was wast-
ing at the schoolhouse, describing the attack with the slate and sug-
gesting his academic career had come to an end. According to the
autobiography, Thomas Grayson tossed the stack of drawings into
the fire and gave his son a severe scolding. Grayson also immedi-
ately made plans to ship his wayward son north, to St. Mary's of the
Barrens College in Perryville, Missouri, near St. Louis.

During the year he spent in Missouri, the last time he would have
any formal schooling, young A.J. would be transformed by experi-
ence from an idle dreamer drawing into a young man planning real
adventure in the West. With his St. Mary's classmates, he visited the
estate of Pierre Chouteau Jr., one of the founders of St. Louis, who
kept bison and other western wildlife on his land. A.J. decided he had
to see bison in the wild. However he might manage it, he must head
westward with the wagons to California.

Still, that dream would have to wait. When schooling ended, the
only avenue open to young A.J. led home. His father's health was failing,

and even though he had not been close to his parents, the young man felt a responsibility to help. After Thomas Grayson's death, A.J. took his small inheritance to a rough new town called Columbia, Missouri, to establish a general store. A.J. worked hard and learned the basics of running a business. As a result of this formative experience, general stores were nearly always part of A.J.'s enterprises, even years later in California and Mexico when the real estate had come to matter more to his fortune than anything he built upon it.

During his years as a shopkeeper, A.J. met twenty-one-year-old Frances Jane Timmons from Monroe. Their abiding love is described well in the poems he composed to her between meeting and getting married less than six months later. Yet even more about the man is expressed in Frances' later memories. "It was his intention to quit forever the country of his nativity and endeavor to cross the Rocky Mountains and dwell upon the far off Pacific shores," she wrote. In marrying A.J., Frances—and later their son Ned—traded a conventional life for expedition and adventure.

In February of 1846 A.J. placed a notice in the *Saint Louis Weekly Reveille*, beneath the headline "Ho for California!" As was customary for such formal-sounding documents, the notice asserts A.J.'s claims on leadership for a wagon trip westward "to preserve good order while on the route." He proposed to leave from Independence on the Missouri River by April 15 and suggested that prospects arrive with arms and ammunition, reliable mules or oxen and provisions for at least six months.

Through the adventurous months and years that followed, A.J., the wife he usually called "Frank" and the rest of the Graysons did nothing to sever their ties to their place on the Boeuf River that came to be known as Fort Necessity. In the manner of *Gone with the Wind* and other traditional Southern tales, land tells you who you are by reminding you from whence you came. Land, as long as you can retain it, is the home where you can always return. And land, more than any sliding scale of currency, defines your prosperity for your lifetime and for all who come after you.

In 1836, one of A.J.'s older siblings, Wiley Blount Grayson, built an impressive home on the family land. It was to this structure, often called the "big house," that Jack Grayson's father—also named Charles Jackson Grayson—would return with his bride in the early twentieth century. And just down the road a smaller home would be constructed and in which Jack himself would be born. The power of real estate runs throughout the Grayson family story. In fact, A.J.'s greatest wealth came from buying land in a tumbledown bayside settlement called Yerba Buena that he would later help rename San Francisco.

Despite A.J.'s published wishes for "good order while on the route," chaos besieged the company he formed. By the time they set forth on May 12, 1846, into countryside aswarm with immigrant groups heading in the same direction, A.J. was relinquishing his leadership position to W.H. Russell and L.W. Boggs. A.J.'s account and others of that time describe considerable disagreement about virtually every aspect of the trip, including the precise route, the order of wagons, the assignment of tasks, the ever-present dangers of fast-changing weather and, of course, Indian attack. Wagon trains like the one A.J. had taken such effort to organize broke continuously into smaller groups with new leaders.

"Both the Oregon and California emigration traveled together on the Oregon Trail for a long time," A.J. wrote later. "Quite a considerable number who had set out for California changed their minds and determined to go to Oregon. This was on account of our hearing the news that war had been declared between the US and Mexico, and consequently many emigrants were afraid to risk themselves and their families in a hostile country."

These trips west, therefore, became one long series of forks in the road—difficult decisions that might make the difference between life and death. Nothing demonstrated this fact, to A.J. and to others on the trail, more profoundly than the tragedy of the Donner Party who began in the initial wagon train with A.J. A detour took the Donners and several other families across Utah's Wasatch Mountains

and the Great Salt Lake Desert. But the situation worsened when delays meant that, instead of reaching the verdant Sacramento Valley by September, they were climbing into the Sierra Nevada range in November. The deep snows awaiting them forced the wagon train to stop and left the party praying for an early spring.

Thirty-six of the eighty-one members of the Donner Party perished from cold and exposure that winter. Yet what caught the media's attention, both in California and nationally, when survivors straggled in was their tales of cannibalism. Many members ate the flesh of companions who had died—or fed it to the children to keep them alive. These tales sensationally underscored the dangers inherent in the passage west.

In his autobiography, A.J. records the date of the family's arrival in California as October 12, 1846—the place probably near present-day Pilot Hill amidst the Sacramento and Feather River valleys. The place they spent their first night in relative safety became known forever to them as Happy Camp. Years later, after enjoying considerable financial success, A.J. commissioned William S. Jewett to create a painting of the moment. Though a private commission for the family, Jewett's painting that A.J. named "The Promised Land" generated excitement before it even left his studio. The work—showing A.J. in the buckskins he wore with the Society of California Pioneers, Frances, Ned and a fanciful horse plus a freshly slain deer—enjoyed an exciting public debut at the First Industrial Exhibition of the Mechanics Institute in 1857.

The Graysons arrived in California at a politically delicate moment. Rebellious Americans calling themselves the Bear Flag Party were seizing control of land from Mexico. There is no record of A.J. firing at Mexican troops during this tense period, but he did leave Frances and Ned behind for several months to help round up volunteers. He emerged from this effort with the rank of "Colonel," though most such titles were bestowed as mere courtesies rather than actual job descriptions.

With the prospect of peace settling in and Mexican troops moving out, the Graysons could at last ponder what to make of their arrival

The Promised Land by William S. Jewett
A.J. Grayson with Ned and Frances upon arriving in California

in the Promised Land. By February 1847, they were settled into a hotel in Yerba Buena, a settlement of fewer than 500 residents and not even two dozen structures. There were no wharves, but simply a wooden dock at the water's edge where immigrants who had opted for the long voyage around South America could at last set foot on dry land. A.J. quickly engaged with the people with the grandest vision for Yerba Buena, participating in discussions that led to renaming it for the nearby Franciscan mission. From this point forward, the community would be known as San Francisco.

The business of real estate is often a matter of timing and sometimes a matter of luck. A.J. was both wise and fortunate enough to buy a lot from the fifty offered to the members of the California Battalion for twelve dollars each. The spot he chose was on the southeast corner of Broadway and Powell Street, so the house he built with $400-worth of lumber became the first building ever erected on Powell. There are records of the Graysons' first San Francisco home lasting until 1879, but it may well have survived until the earthquake and fire of 1906. In his faith in real estate, whether in the city of San

Francisco or later in Marin County or San Jose, property that in to-day's market would be worth hundreds of millions, A.J. was a true forerunner of Jack who fended off the "why take the risk?" cautions he heard in his many endeavors.

Everything in and about the city changed on March 15, 1848, the day *The Californian* reported the discovery of gold at Captain John Sutter's sawmill. A.J. himself quickly decided that the work of going after the stuff was simply too hard. Yet gold, and the thousands of new settlers it attracted, made his fortune all the same. Within a year, San Francisco had 135 completed buildings plus ten more homes under construction. Within that same year, A.J.'s stores and other ventures had made him one of the growing city's wealthiest men. He purchased 200 acres (later known as The Thicket) where the city of Fairfax now stands in Marin County. He even won election to the District Legislature in February of 1849.

The rise and fall of fortunes are always interesting tales, and we do see the Graysons stumble badly first with the end of the California Gold Rush and then with the severe economic decline of 1851. Eventually, A.J. joined the line to file for bankruptcy, retaining of his riches only a few items placed in his wife's name and a few bits of real estate outside the city, including the Marin County property they came to use as a retreat.

After something less than a year of life on their farm, they sold the place and used the money to make a fresh start—it later became known as Fairfax Manor and was owned by the man behind the popular Woodward's Gardens, an open-air amusement park in San Francisco. In addition, with the economy's recovery, the Graysons' holdings in the city started generating significant rents again. There was money to travel a bit, including a trip home to visit the relatives in Fort Necessity. And there was money for A.J., upon returning with his wife and son in San Francisco, to give up the day-to-day drag of commerce and concentrate on the exploring and hunting that were his great passions.

"The river is deep and tranquil," he wrote from one journey,

seemingly overwhelmed by impressions. "I could not describe the innumerable quantity of water fowl and the large herds of elk. But of every description of water fowl my pen could scarcely describe the numbers or the excitement they would create in the breast of a sportsman…These and a thousand other birds mingling their songs together create the indescribable sensation of pleasure that can only be felt by one fond of nature in its wildest and most beautiful forms."

The main instigator of the new life that would earn A.J. renown as the "Audubon of the West" was his wife. It's unclear what Frances thought that day gazing at a "double-elephant" folio edition of Audubon's landmark *Birds of America*. And she couldn't turn to A.J. and tell him, since he was away on one of his hunting trips. Perhaps he had told her of his early fascination with art, of the fracas with his long-ago teacher in Fort Necessity. Perhaps he had shown her some few bits of drawing or painting, new or leftover from childhood. But gazing at Audubon's birds two years after the artist's death, she saw something that she would encourage her husband to pursue.

By 1853, the Graysons had moved from north to south of San Francisco Bay, settling on four acres in San Jose and building a house and garden they called Bird's Nest Cottage, so Ned could attend Santa Clara Mission, which eventually became Santa Clara University. And using a set of watercolors he had bought for Ned, A.J. could teach himself to paint. He cobbled together a technique of quickly sketching birds in the wild, then applying a light color wash and finally using a dry brush for strokes of strong color. A.J. was persuaded to enter three of his pictures in the California State Fair in 1855, taking home first place and a silver cup. A drawing of a roadrunner was his first published work, the first of eighteen drawings to appear in *Hutchings' California Magazine* in 1857 and 1858.

Although Frances remained A.J.'s devoted wife until he drew his last breath, it was about this time that the man took a passionate mistress—the Smithsonian Institution. No single professional relationship contributed to A.J.'s last reputation as an Audubon-style naturalist and artist more than the scientific organization based in

Black Vented Oriole by Andrew Jackson Grayson
(Birds of the Pacific Slope)

the nation's capital. In a flourish that would become impossible only a few years later, he simply wrote a letter to the Smithsonian and volunteered his services as a collector in the field.

Part of A.J.'s motivation was pragmatic: he quickly realized that without any background in ornithology, he was painting birds as they appeared to him, without understanding of how they actually functioned. The Smithsonian would be an important resource. A.J. couldn't have realized it at the time, but the institution was then the domain of America's greatest nineteenth century ornithologist, Spencer Fullerton Baird. It was Baird who would accept A.J.'s offer, letting him become one of the last naturalists to record wildlife in the wild rather than, as was already becoming the norm, amid dusty collections in offices and academies. Mexico and California would serve as A.J.'s research, collection and artistic turf until his death in Mazatlán in 1869. Frances lived on until 1909.

A.J.'s legacy faded into obscurity for more than a century, waiting for rediscovery in the archives of the University of California's

Bancroft Library. Finally in 1982, Andrew Hoyem of San Francisco's Arion Press heard of the works and decided to explore the possibility of publishing *Birds of the Pacific Slope*. He did this with enormous assistance from zoologist Lois Chambers Stone, who had researched A.J.'s life and work. Best of all, the latest technologies of the time made reproducing the natural wonders seen and captured by Andrew Jackson Grayson a practical reality.

The message of this exciting development—mining the wisdom, work and perseverance of the past by using the latest tools—was not lost upon A.J.'s great-great-great-nephew, another Jack Grayson growing up on the same bend in the road that had already sent out one of its own to life's unpredictable adventures.

BIRDS OF THE PACIFIC SLOPE BY ANDREW JACKSON GRAYSON

Black-Bellied Whistling Duck

Black-Collared Hawk

Common Moorhen

Military Macaw

2

FORT NECESSITY

BORN ON THE GRAYSON FAMILY LAND IN 1923, "Charlie Jack" Grayson grew up without knowledge of his famous ancestor—largely because no one currently living knew who Andrew Jackson Grayson had been or what he had accomplished until Jack's cousin started researching. Since A.J. had gone off to California to make and lose his fortune, the Graysons remained close to home and close to the land. They thrived by maintaining an agricultural system that may strike some today as feudal or worse. Yet like any economic system able to remain in place for decades or even centuries, tenant farming—or sharecropping—must have provided benefits on both sides of the equation.

The system was important and perhaps essential to survival in the Deep South. At its simplest, it required two components: a landowner, who often expanded holdings ten or twenty acres at a time as opportunities arose, and laborers with a strong back and few employment opportunities other than small-scale agriculture. In return for being allowed to live and farm on the landowner's property, the tenant farmer—sharecropper—paid rent. Often, rather than cash, he would return a portion of his crop to the landowner as barter.

As was common, there was a general store on the Grayson land, where tenants could purchase supplies against their account, to be paid when the crops came in. Although the system may seem strange today, sharecropping survived because a farmer with no land cannot

feed a family, and the economics of farming before industrial agriculture took over demanded significant numbers of laborers.

"My views about life," Jack says, "come from my early life—before age fourteen—on a farm, in a tightly connected rural community, during depression years, with seasons of life and death on the farm—in people, animals, crops. If things didn't work out, there was always rebirth in next year's crop, in children, in forgetting and moving on, in forgiving, accepting not fighting nature, living with disappointments. My father seldom complained, always forgave, accepted disappointments as part of success, and moved on."

Jack's father was controlled and in charge, as his life demanded that he be at all times. As one of eight children living under Louisiana's pre-determined Napoleonic Code, Charles Jackson Grayson Sr., Jack's father, inherited his one-eighth share of his father's land, 360 acres, and soon after that started accumulating more. When he first brought his bride, Daphne de Graffenreid, home to Fort Necessity, they lived in a portion of the big house built by Wiley Grayson in 1836, after a while building and moving into a smaller place built from cypress across the road. By the time he died, "Mistuh Charlie," as he was known to all, had a spread of about 3000 acres, all of it housing families and all of it producing income.

Sharing its name with one of the few battles George Washington lost during the American Revolution, Fort Necessity (which today has a population of about fifteen) developed in what now is Franklin Parish but once included parts of Ouachita and Catahoula. Nearby Fort Miro, later Monroe, was the only settlement of any size in Louisiana north of the line running from Natchitoches to Natchez on the high bluffs across the river in Mississippi. The majority of its settlers were similar to the Graysons of Kentucky. Of Scottish, Scotch-Irish or English descent, they moved to the area from older states like Virginia and the Carolinas. They found something to settle for in the rich, dark, alluvial soil of Franklin, only one parish removed from the Mississippi River. And they found much, culturally and religiously, to distinguish themselves from the mostly Roman Catholic French

speakers of Louisiana farther to the south.

Fort Necessity was located at the approximate location of Boeuf Prairie, first capital of the parish, growing from a group of farmers who in 1881, according to local tradition, got tired of traveling all the way to the parish seat of Winnsboro to get their mail. A post office, they declared, was a "necessity," and the name for the settlement apparently caught on. In a brief history of Franklin Parish compiled in 1937 under the Works Progress Administration, author Blanche Oliver describes a scene in which the young Jack Grayson would feel right at home:

> The 'cabin in the cotton' is a pleasing picture of reality, particularly in the season when the bolls have burst and the fleecy staple hangs in snowy clusters from the stalks. On the larger plantations, usually near the road, tenant cabins of two to five rooms are often grouped together, each surrounded by a picket fence, and presenting the appearance of an island in a sea of green or white depending on the season.

Though Charlie Jack understood the situation imperfectly, if at all, as a child, his parents offered him the first great human mystery of the many he would encounter in his long life. He was an only child, meaning that their relationship with him was a daily reality, as was their relationship with each other. It is unclear whether he ever took on their problems or wondered if he somehow was to blame.

In retrospect, Jack describes his childhood as "ninety percent very happy," clearly a percentage that many remembering their own early years would wish for. He certainly enjoyed life on the farm or at least remembers it with warmth, whether that meant getting up at three in the morning to fire up the steam engine that ran the cotton gin or simply living day to day with no running water, no electricity, no inside toilet, no heat in the winter or air conditioning in the summer and no ice except for that dropped off by a truck that came from Winnsboro twice a week. Throughout his earliest years, the

only "machine" used in farming was a mule, which gave way later to the family's first tractor known as "Ol' Peg."

Jack's mother had grown up in the "big city" of Shreveport, daughter of a family originally from Bern, Switzerland, and took for granted luxuries like electricity and plumbing—two of many luxuries she would not have in the early years of her marriage at Fort Necessity. She met Charles at the college now known as Louisiana Tech in Ruston, earning her teaching certificate after he had dropped out to return to the family farm. Eventually, she got her first teaching job in south Louisiana, surrounded by French-speaking Cajuns. By all accounts, Daphne enjoyed being a teacher. But that didn't stop her from letting her heart overrule her head when Charles traveled down from Fort Necessity to ask her to marry him. In those days, marrying meant "whither thou goest," and with Charles, that meant the sharecropped land around his family place.

Charles Grayson had no fewer than seventy-seven houses on his land, and that meant seventy-seven families depended on him for their ability to feed themselves. This produced a complicated relationship in which tenant farmers were at the same time dependents, business partners, employees and members of an extended family. Everything that was decided on the farm—who got what land and how much, who paid what percentage of his crop, who got credit at the general store—Charles decided. Yet that same power over lives made him a paternalistic figure to all, called in to solve problems, give advice on equipment and growing techniques, and, often late at night, settle money disputes, bail workers out of jail, pay their hospital bills and pacify marital spats. A certain kind of bravery would have been necessary to do those things in the settings they required Charles to enter, but there never seemed to be a moment's hesitation. Charlie Jack came to admire that aspect of his father, even if he was also the imposing man gazing down from the horse.

There were two basic types of sharecroppers living on the Grayson land: those who could afford to own farm equipment and those who could not. That ability came to mean everything, since it directly

affected how productive a plot of land could hope to be for everyone involved. People without equipment were allowed to farm only six to eight acres, as that was all they could manage. People with equipment (mules as well as simple mechanical devices) were entrusted with a maximum of twenty acres. The first group had to pay the Graysons half of their crop, while the second had to give up only one-fourth to recognize their investment in the business. In general, Jack remembers, those with more invested worked harder, lived more responsibly and gave up on the land less easily or quickly. It was a lesson in the world's economic functioning that was not lost on young Jack.

Jack clearly remembers spending considerable amounts of his time as a boy visiting adults and playing with children in the tenant houses. He found his place naturally among the "porch children" (small enough to stay home all day) and the "yard children" (old enough to go exploring and pal around with their peers). Jack even slept over many nights, not wishing to stop playing to go home to his far more comfortable bed close to his parents. On Sundays, virtually all the tenants attended a Baptist church Jack's father had built for them. It was the "colored church" as clearly as their cemetery on the land was the "colored cemetery." There were lines that no one dared cross. But that didn't prevent Charlie Jack from sitting out on the grass and listening to the glorious singing pouring forth from every church window.

And then there was Teenie. Call her a nanny in the British tradition or call her Mammy in the vocabulary of the Old South, Teenie was, according to Jack, "the family cook, house cleaner, child watcher, surrogate mother and best friend I ever had." The boy viewed Teenie as an eternal optimist who was never angry and always laughing, and he sought her love and approval with great intensity. The two played games indoors and out, and they even went crawfishing together, tracking down the little towers of mud on the ground that surely had "mudbugs" inside. Teenie had a man living with her for a time and that man became a kind of surrogate parent as well, taking Jack places and showing him things, explaining the way life

Jack and Teenie

and people and animals and equipment worked. Though Jack's own father called Jack "Partner"—"Podnuh"—with some affection, it's obvious with hindsight that Teenie and her man gave the boy a different form of partnership.

When Teenie died suddenly of a heart attack, Jack had his first introduction to losing a parent. He attended her funeral at the "colored church" and broke into sobs at her burial service. In life, she had often punctuated the minutes and hours by telling Jack, "Let's get on up de big road"—but now, he realized, she had done so without him and would never return. In a book Jack later wrote at Harvard, he offered these words as tribute: "Teenie Williams—one of the finest persons I shall ever hope to know in my entire life... Perhaps only those from the Deep South can truly understand when I say I hope to pass along to my children the philosophy, the depth of her understanding and most of all—the laughter she gave my life."

As he grew in the direction of manhood in Fort Necessity—and

Jack and his red wagon

toward a life to be lived as Jack Grayson, not Charlie Jack—the young man's education progressed on at least two fronts: one educational, thanks to schools built near his family's farm, and the other agricultural. The latter included not only the countless details of farming, from crops to soil to climate, but also the business of making a living off the land. Jack's father and mother believed passionately in both educational fronts.

School was a catch-as-catch-can affair and even included Jack's own mother eventually serving as his teacher. When Jack entered the classroom for the first time—a place he would spend a good deal of time over the next eight-plus decades and develop some of his better ideas—that "classroom" was a two-room schoolhouse about a mile from his house in which his mother taught grades five through eleven. His closest boyhood friend's mother taught grades one through four, which is naturally where he learned that era's three *R*s—reading, writing and 'rithmetic. At the end of his second-grade year, the parish decided to roll the schoolhouse along the road on logs and move

A young Jack Grayson

it five miles into the town of Fort Necessity. The town in those days had three buildings—a store, a post office and an all-important cotton gin—and a population of twenty-two. Jack would be bumped ahead a year twice, based on his handling of the materials. He finished "high school," which in those days ended with eleventh grade, at the age of fifteen.

Of the thirteen graduating class members of Fort Necessity High School (a record number at that time), Jack's best friend was John "Bubba" Daily, who lived about a mile down the road. The boys had grown up together in the tradition of Huck Finn and Tom Sawyer: grabbing their slingshots, BB guns or twelve- and twenty-gauge shotguns to hunt anything that moved. They fished and swam in—and sometimes even drank from—the muddy Boeuf River, camped out, rode horses at high speed, fired off multitudes of firecrackers, built model airplanes and exchanged the secret codes encouraged by Little Orphan Annie rings. In fact, the boys' first long separation occurred when Bubba went with the Army to Europe and Jack went with the Navy to the Pacific during World War II. Bubba would spend his

Ft. Necessity graduating class: Jack 4th from the left, front row

career in oil and gas and retire. By the time both men turned ninety, they would still phone each other, laugh about old times and admit they never expected to stick around quite so long.

Jack's education was hardly limited to a schoolhouse, no matter how many or few rooms it had. Though his parents, as he remembered them, read no books, knew no classic literature and never seemed to regret it, Jack plunged into the world of popular adventure. Reading by the fire at night or outside on the porch swing in daylight, he came to live the lives of Dick Tracy, Tom Swift and Bomba the Jungle Boy. His heroes faced challenges and adversities, often in the form of colorful villains, and they always triumphed. Jack's world view emerged from these daily readings, his basic and foundational optimism that many would classify as distinctly American. This message was bolstered as Jack listened to the family radio at night, when the channels tended to clear and a signal made it to Fort Necessity through the static.

One of his favorites on the radio was *Dick Tracy*, helped in the fight for justice in the universe by *Buck Rogers*, *Jack Armstrong* and

the *Green Hornet*. At the Graysons', and elsewhere as the American economy slid into the Great Depression, *Little Orphan Annie* delivered her message of simplistic optimism over the airwaves and in her daily newspaper comic strips. There were music programs as well, big bands usually, fronted by the likes of Glenn Miller, the Dorsey brothers and Benny Goodman.

Most of these shows that connected the Graysons and young Jack in particular to a larger world would be classified as escape—something America needed and embraced with enthusiasm in those dark days. But one thing Jack remembers that was not an escape was the radio presence of President Franklin Roosevelt. These Fireside Chats dared to look the Depression in the eye, promised little except hard work and austerity and still managed to exude the faith that America was a great country that would recover. While sitting with his parents beside their radio, young Jack began to understand that communicating a vision mattered.

Education took many forms on the Grayson farm. Lessons were all present and pressing, and they existed in the fields, at the markets or among the houses of sharecroppers rather than in a book. In the same manner that Jack's mother was his primary teacher at school, his father taught him the lessons of the farm. He never pressured Jack to choose farming as his permanent occupation, but he certainly made it clear that Graysons of the past had made their living off the land. As an only child under the Napoleonic Code, there could be little doubt that the farm his parents had developed would be his someday. It was Jack's job to understand its workings—agricultural, social and financial—to the degree that he could carry it forward to the next generation. It was the Southern way.

At this point, Mr. Bea Fred came into his life. Mr. Bea Fred was assigned to be Jack's "buddy" or more importantly his "safety" in the fields. He taught Jack many basic skills such as how to ride a horse and rope a calf. Jack views Mr. Bea Fred's daily role, like Teenie's, as quite important to his development in those formative years from age six through fifteen.

Mr. Bea Fred, a longtime friend of the Grayson family

Work on the farm began early. Young boys like Jack were soon drafted into milking cows, slopping hogs, feeding chickens, shucking corn for horses, pumping water from the well, chopping weeds in the garden, spreading poison to protect tomato plants from bugs, digging up potatoes and thumping watermelons to gauge their ripeness. Additionally, one of Jack's important jobs was driving a horse drawn wagon around the sharecroppers' plots and gathering up cotton to take it to the gin. Once there, the boy would let a steam-driven "sucker" take the cotton from the wagon, cut out the seeds with whirling saws and finally press the cleaned, fluffy cotton into bales. His wagon empty, Jack would head on to collect the next sharecropper's cotton.

Watching his father ride through half his holdings one day and the other half the next, Jack came to glimpse what his own life here would be like—he was his father's "Podnuh," after all. In time he acquired his own horses and his own dogs to accompany him into the fields, animals with names like Peanut Butter, Potato Chips, Sport and Buddy. Jack relied on them to help him round up the farm's 700 cattle for branding or for dipping, when they got their hides covered

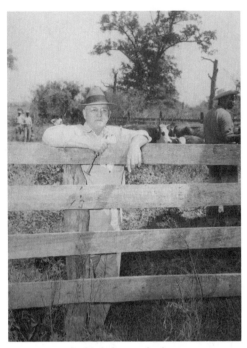

Jack's father on the farm

in smelly creosote to ward off flies. He came to love riding from one end of the property to the other, taking on more and more of the roles his father handled. He particularly enjoyed full-speed rides through the woods with his friend Bubba. Being knocked to the ground from time to time did nothing to curtail this enthusiasm, the enjoyment of motion and sunshine and open air. As years passed, around the farm, especially among the tenant families, he became not the little kid on the porch or in the yard but the patriarch-in-waiting sitting high up on horseback. To this degree, his father's lessons on life around Fort Necessity were coming through loud and clear.

In addition to learning a very hard business, Jack was also piling up impressions his parents could not have imagined. Memories of childhood, of course, but also reactions, feelings and observations. Not the stuff of the farmer at all. The stuff of someone no one would expect to find among them. A writer. Jack's papers include at least three unpublished short stories about Fort Necessity, written as he

was testing his wings, teaching himself the difficult task of making meaning and order from the living things around him. In time he would dream bigger dreams, set in places like Paris and starring literary heroes like Hemingway. In the beginning, though, his world was far from Paris.

Jack penned a detail-rich story from memory titled "General Store" and an eerie vignette titled "The Wardrobe Key" about the night his beloved grandmother died. Most significantly, in nine other typed pages, Jack lets us enter what must have been the central internal debate of his early life. "Trapped" tells of a youth's reluctance to set aside his childhood diminutive of "Charlie Jack" to be "Mistuh Charlie." How could such a change happen so fast, the protagonist of the story wonders, when he is so not ready to "be" his father? The drought-dry summer on the farm that's now his gives cause to one extended passage of self-examination:

> He reached down, crumbled a brittle clod of dirt between his fingers and watched it sift away in a dull-gray cloud. It drifted like the truck dust and then suddenly shot up like a dust-devil on a shaft of heat into the blaze of the empty summer sky and sun. Another scorcher. He knew it wouldn't rain. Of course not. But what was he going to do? Curse God? The earth was his mother and his casket. Curse his father? Curse farming? Who was he going to blame it on?

Of the few young people around Fort Necessity who bothered to finish high school, even fewer entertained the idea of college. Yet both of Jack's parents felt he should go. For his mother, college would be what took him away from this place, presumably forever. For his father, college would help him manage this land better, understanding the new farm technologies being invented and the new financial models being developed. For Jack, college was something else again, perhaps something that combined both his parents' wishes and added his own dreams of adventure, exotic travel, danger and triumph.

The day finally came for Charles and Daphne Grayson to drive their son to Atlanta so he could begin studies at Georgia Military Academy (GMA), the school they agreed would be best for their fifteen-year-old after perusing brochures from all sorts of schools. New Orleans had been quickly and explicitly ruled out: Too wild. Too laissez-faire. And too much of a Sin City. His parents believed a military-style discipline in Georgia would be good for their only child. Despite fears of everything that was new, Charlie Jack vowed to give both the school and its discipline his best effort, from its uniforms to its drilling to its mock wars fought around campus. Saturday afternoons quickly became the highlight of Jack's week, as he would find a way to indulge in his newfound passion for White Castle hamburgers. There had been no restaurants around Fort Necessity at all.

"'I know you'll do your best,' my father said before leaving me," Jack recalls. "That's about all the instructions I got. But I made a promise to myself. I was not going to call my parents and tell them I wanted to come home. I didn't want to disappoint them."

3

HIGHER EDUCATION

T HE FOUR YEARS THAT FOLLOWED JACK'S departure to Georgia Military Academy (GMA) in 1939 helped him put away the child who was Charlie Jack forever. His single post-graduate year at GMA, followed by three years at Tulane University in New Orleans where he earned his business degree, accomplished, essentially, what his parents hoped they would. They gave the young man time to find his own footing in the world, far from the fertile soil and limited horizons of Fort Necessity. In ways Jack still grapples with, however, making it to Tulane required that he survive that year at GMA—a place where the horrors of war he would later experience in the Pacific were foreshadowed by the hazing.

The school began as the Georgia Military Academy in 1900. Today, Woodward Academy in College Park, Georgia, is a day-student, co-educational private school that reflects little or nothing of its past as a boarding program. Like most private schools, Woodward stresses the individual words of its motto—Excellence, Character and Opportunity. The same words, could, presumably, be applied to the military academy founded in 1900 by Colonel John Charles Woodward. The surrounding community must have believed in Woodward's vision, too, since they sold him sixteen acres with a non-interest-bearing loan of $1500 to be repaid "when possible."

In a postcard from the period Jack attended, Col. Woodward's vision looks much like many visions of the gracious and glorious Old

South: a tall and imposing red-brick Founders Hall gazing out over a wide, grassy parade ground with an American flag waving high above it. Most intriguing, what appear to be Civil War-era cannons are positioned around the building, as though the staff and students inside the hall were preparing for yet another Yankee assault. Only hinted at, touching and stretching beyond the edge of the frame, are the barracks and mess halls that would fill so much of Jack's year at GMA. It was there that GMA sought to provide, and enforce, what it saw as a "well-ordered, sympathetic but strictly guarded home life for the cadets." Formed primarily of boys who had been there for several years and were hazed upon their arrival, they were entitled by tradition to create misery for first year students, called rats. And despite its apparent commitment to the contrary, GMA and its instructors—some of whom remembered their own vicious hazing as plebes at West Point—did nothing to stop them.

From the first day of school, Jack did what all the new boys did, for that was the military way—enforcing at the time his dislike and distrust of the military way. He was given his uniforms, gray for dress and drill and blue fatigue for ordinary wear, and immediately taught the basics of marching everywhere, whether to class or to church. Each Sunday the entire Cadet Corps was made to parade and work through all its rifle routines for the inspiration and entertainment of parents, relatives, girlfriends and any visiting dignitaries. The cadets also paraded along Peachtree Street in Atlanta from time to time and even (though not during the year Jack was there) in inaugural parades through Washington, DC.

Perhaps strikingly, for a school that pressed its cadets so hard, GMA also attempted to cultivate their softer, more cultural sides. Surely remembering the reality, or at least the illusion, of the Confederacy that Atlanta so revered, the school actually taught its boys to be gentlemen, making sure they behaved through Old World tea every afternoon and knew at least the rudiments of socializing, attending concerts and dancing. Jack's skills in the latter activity would serve as his sole happy memory of the year.

Georgia Military Academy

The hazing, however, was another matter entirely. Though such practices were tolerated in many military-school settings, from West Point to Texas A&M (which had endured more than one national hazing scandal in the 1920s), they took on a particularly sharp edge at GMA. To some military minds, Jack recalls, hazing seemed to exist as a way to establish hierarchy, exert discipline and encourage toughness. Though he established no close friendships while at GMA, Jack did feel united with many of his fellow victims.

Typically, as for anyone being held hostage, the raids began at night. Shortly after Jack and his peers had drifted off to sleep in their bunks, their abusers would enter the barracks loudly and violently, driving and dumping sleeping boys from their beds. Hits and kicks quickly became commonplace, as did the practice of making the new boys bend to the floor, grab hold of their genitals and endure a beating with a host of wooden objects. Any boy unwise enough to break into tears or attempt to escape was made to suffer doubly in the next attack. And it was understood among the boys that it would be

disgraceful, not to mention dangerous, to squeal to parents or school authorities. This tyranny, mixed with Jack's own fear of disappointing his parents, ensured that his mouth remained shut, for the rest of his year at GMA and indeed for the remainder of his parents' lives.

A particularly devastating form of hazing involved locking a group of rats in a room and letting them fight it out, punching and kicking, until there was a "last man standing." To not fight was to choose an even worse beating, so whatever their feelings about the exercise, most boys fought hard and some fought dirty—for there was no referee to decide fair or foul. It was brutal, Jack remembers, and ultimately vicious. In the spirit of such novels as *Lord of the Flies* and *Sands of the Kalahari,* he found himself pondering just how violent otherwise-peaceful human beings could be—how close to a Darwinian jungle our world is. Years later, as a scholar, Jack would read of many group behavior studies that made the same point. He couldn't read a single set of results without remembering his dark days and even darker nights, some spent awake in his bunk fearing the next attack, at Georgia Military Academy.

It is emblematic of all Jack endured at GMA that he remembers very little about it—no particular friends, no favorite instructors, no subjects that handed him a fresh way to view the world. He simply figures that he went to classes, did his homework and passed from one thing to the next with fairly good grades. Indeed, the only military academy experience he recalls with more than a little pleasure occurred in December of 1939, before he returned to Fort Necessity for Christmas.

The Atlanta world premiere of *Gone with the Wind* included cadets from GMA ceremoniously lined up along what must have been a red carpet. Though remarkably un-star struck—and familiar with only Clark Gable among the stars—Jack enjoyed seeing Gable, Vivien Leigh and Olivia de Havilland climb from their limousines and enter the Loew's Grand Theater via the protection he and his classmates were providing. Leslie Howard passed on attending the premiere, having returned to his native England with the outbreak of

World War II. Hattie McDaniel and the film's other black performers could not attend because of Atlanta's Jim Crow laws of that time. Decades later, Georgia-born President Jimmy Carter would call the premiere, which attracted upwards of a million people, "the biggest event to happen in the South in my lifetime."

Jack doesn't recall seeing the actual movie that night, though the GMA contingent was presumably invited to do so, but he does remember an Old South ball held immediately after the screening. In full dress grays that recalled the Confederacy, Jack was both willing and able to tap his predecessor on the shoulder—a gesture called cutting—and spend a few memorable if fleeting moments circling the dance floor with none other than Scarlett O'Hara.

If Jack had felt the least bit comfortable about telling his parents about the hazing at GMA, Christmas break would have been his best opportunity. But he didn't. In addition to the imposed pressures of not wanting to be a squealer and the certainty of retribution once back on campus, two other things made sure that the young man's lips remained sealed. One was his fear of seeming a weakling, even to his parents, who presumably knew him better and loved him more. The other was the graphic aspect of some of the punishments. In an era that encouraged young people to tiptoe around subjects of a sexual nature, Jack would have found it difficult to talk about the hazing, even had he wanted to.

Mostly, he talked with his parents about college. Though they had been reluctant to send the boy off on his own to New Orleans after eleventh grade, his maturing at GMA made Tulane University their choice for him now. They passed over the nearer college they had attended, feeling the boy needed a better education that would allow him to see a bit more of the world. And more interestingly, they passed over Louisiana State University in the state capital of Baton Rouge. Only a decade earlier, Governor and later US Senator Huey P. Long had poured resources into "his" university, adding buildings and hiring respected professors from all over the country. Long, who was assassinated in 1935 as he walked through the Capitol building

he built—inspiring one of the professors he had recruited, Robert Penn Warren, to write *All the King's Men*—went a step further on behalf of LSU. He arranged the finances so children of Louisiana residents could attend virtually free. As Tulane was a private school that charged significant tuition, Jack's parents' decision to send him there was quite a statement.

Jack remembers little about his GMA graduation. He was mostly happy to leave, insisting decades later that typing was the only skill he picked up there that did him much good as a professional. GMA resembles a limbo in his life, a place he went for a brief time in between two other worlds. Tulane provided a coming-of-age in a life that still, by later standards, managed to be largely innocent of the forces of the larger world.

The most important story of Jack Grayson's three years at Tulane University, studying in what was then called the College of Commerce, is told in the changing nature of the *Jambalaya*, the school yearbook. The edition for 1940, the year he entered as a freshman, looks like most college yearbooks from any time in history—two leather covers binding oversized glossy pages of formal portraits of students and professors in stacked rows, juxtaposed with candid, smiling shots of kids at football games, dances and other aspects of campus life. Opening images show the university's ivy-covered buildings and a big band, of the sort that played the music Jack loved from listening to the radio in Fort Necessity. Leslie J. Buchan is identified as Dean of the College of Commerce, and a young man named Kendall H. Cram is featured as the school's graduate manager of student activities.

In the *Jambalaya* covering Jack's junior year, only two years later, Cram and twenty-one other students are honored for making "the supreme sacrifice in defense of their country." In the 1943 yearbook, the one in which Jack the graduating senior appears three times, all things are different. The *Jambalaya* has taken on a new title just inside the cover: Tulane at War. Indeed, there are so many photos of young men in Navy uniforms in the volume that any other style of dress seems out of place.

Jack was part of Tulane's Navy ROTC program, a high level known as V-12 that was established on 150 university campuses to produce the officers America's fighting forces needed so desperately. The focus on military training at Tulane was so complete that the *Jambalaya* lists the daily V-12 schedule, from reveille at 6:30 to lights out at 22:00, with calisthenics, classes and study in between. In addition to Jack's appearances with his class and his fraternity, he appears with the ROTC's Second Company identified as "first P.O. officer."

While the *Jambalaya* evokes America's transformation from peacetime to wartime, it only tells a small portion of Jack's story at Tulane. For one thing, coming to the university meant living in what for him was a big city, a New Orleans still aglow with its position as international port and culture capital of the South. For another, it meant living on his own in a manner he never had before. As Tulane did not have dormitories, students were expected to find rooms in a collection of boarding houses scattered through the tree-shaded Uptown section.

The boarding house Jack and his parents chose before his first year featured three rooms with two male students each, plus a fourth room featuring a young woman who lived alone. Jack, the country boy who'd never been much of anywhere, found himself rooming with a fellow named Nigel Rafferty, whose father was a well-to-do doctor in Pass Christian on the Mississippi Gulf Coast. Knowing Nigel opened new windows for Jack. His roommate had a convertible at school with him, meaning they could ride around New Orleans like royalty, seeing the sights that still fascinate tourists. Some weekends, they would head back to Pass Christian, where there were tennis courts in the family's backyard and a sailboat waiting in the Mississippi Sound. And as Jack was a much better student than Nigel, he was able to repay some of the favors by helping his roommate get better grades.

Mealtime at the boarding house was a learning experience all by itself. Against the food-crazed backdrop of New Orleans, night after night Jack saw dishes set in front of him that he had never tasted or even heard of before. If a dish wasn't part of the Southern country

cooking tradition, it hadn't been served in Fort Necessity or even on the outskirts of Atlanta. Here, though, were the seafood wonders of the salty Gulf of Mexico and its tangle of brackish bays. Jack remembers his first encounter with raw oysters, a food he never learned to like, and also strange vegetables like artichokes and Brussels sprouts. Jack never did take to many of the more exotic foods he was served with his fellow housemates, not least because dishes tended to be spicier in the Creole and Cajun traditions than anything he had grown up eating. As an adult, Jack Grayson would travel the world and taste dishes few of his contemporaries would ever even see; but deep down, his preferred cuisine remained simple country cooking.

There was an additional aspect of mealtime at the boarding house, and that was the chance to see their female housemate. Her name was Elizabeth, and while she didn't seem noticeably older than the college students around her, she was far more interesting. Although what she did was a little vague, it was understood she worked for the FBI. In America of 1940, her role suggested *G Men* and *The Untouchables*, Eliot Ness and the then-young J. Edgar Hoover. It meant danger, excitement. Elizabeth seemed all those things and more to the boys sharing the house with her, except that Jack now laughs that she was probably only a secretary. The fact that she had this exotic grownup life, and the fact that she was beautiful, ignited many a dream in each of the boys. Only Jack, however, ended up dating Elizabeth, even talking for a time about marriage.

Even as Jack and Nigel lived happily enough at the boarding house, with nights for cruising New Orleans by convertible and weekends for tennis and sailing on the Mississippi Coast, there was the matter of fraternities. Unlike many college campuses that have frat houses on campus or at the very edge of academic buildings, Tulane had fraternity buildings strewn among the private homes of Uptown New Orleanians. Each house attempted to snag whom they considered the best men for their membership rolls. Since Nigel had already pledged, he wanted his roommate to come along too. This dynamic led to a fateful encounter at the New Orleans Country Club.

One night, as fraternity rush was picking up steam, Nigel's fraternity, Beta Theta Pi, invited Jack and the rest of that year's rushees to a kind of dinner dance in a private room at the country club—a place famous for its old money and insistence on proper decorum. At least Jack had figured out that much, realizing he was entering a world he had never experienced before, enjoying that youthful thrill of anticipation and dread. It wasn't long, though, before the dread started taking over. Almost as soon as he entered the room, he was pressed toward the bar and told to order a drink. Which meant, he figured, a Coca-Cola. Which meant, to them, bourbon and Coke. Jack drank what he was given and thought he'd be going to hell.

Still, if Jack felt he might get off with a warning from the Almighty someday about drinking bourbon, the ten strippers the fraternity brought in from Bourbon Street struck him as another matter altogether. Peer pressure meant he had to keep looking as the women peeled off and squirmed out of piece after piece of clothing, until they stood naked in front of their all-male audience. Then, wearing nothing, each of the strippers made their way to a nervous rushee and settled onto his lap. With his quiet, even naive life so far, Jack was extremely uncomfortable. His shyness around girls had been an issue all along, keeping him from asking them out on dates with the seeming nonchalance he saw among other young men. And now, having never even seen a naked woman, he had one sitting on his lap. Jack was sure he was going to hell now, but at the same time, things were becoming increasingly more interesting. As he remembers the experience, Jack got away from the country club late that night as quickly as he could, later joining another fraternity that had the good sense to ask him what he wanted to do. Jack asked them to take him to a movie. To Nigel's extreme disappointment, Delta Tau Delta had its man.

Classes at Tulane were relatively easy for Jack, as demonstrated by his ability and willingness to tutor his roommate. Subjects were heavily weighted toward a projected life in business, including accounting—something Jack hated, even though he'd later become a

certified public accountant. There were only limited intrusions of social studies and liberal arts into the business curriculum, but the young man enjoyed whatever intrusions he got. He loved the expanded freedom to study and research things that simply interested him, beyond the narrow confines of high school and military academy. For one project, he chose to research and write about the Aztecs of ancient Mexico, finding himself horrified and fascinated by the thousands they sacrificed in their bloody religious ceremonies. For another, he chose Stendahl's classic novel *The Red and the Black*, feeling perhaps for the first time great literature's ability to transport readers to a new world.

But still, in every waking moment, there was the war.

Jack remembers hearing about the United States' entry into the war on the radio while he was playing pinball. Ever since the Japanese attack on Pearl Harbor on December 7, 1941, he knew that, short of a miracle, he'd be called to fight. The news from the European and Pacific theaters was bad throughout much of his time at Tulane. There was a very real awareness that America could lose the war, an awareness that drove so much of Jack's ROTC training. There were even instructors in the program who had been badly burned at Pearl Harbor. They provided a daily reminder of the dangers of real, as opposed to theoretical, combat.

"Pearl Harbor was enough of a disaster," Jack recalls. "But then there was Guadalcanal, which convinced us there would be no quick and easy ending. Plus, there was Hitler, moving west across Europe and forcing the rescue of British troops by sea at Dunkirk. I was beginning to believe it was possible I'd be going to war. I didn't really think I was going to die, but I got scared a lot. I had no idea about my future."

The tentative quality forced upon all young men likely to serve wrote the final chapter to Jack's romance with Elizabeth. The two had been a serious item through at least the final years of college, with him going home to meet her parents on the north shore of Lake Pontchartrain and entertaining the idea of marriage. In his core,

though, Jack felt too immature to take such a big step, even if he wasn't sure how to break that news to Elizabeth—or, for that matter, to her parents, who were pressing the young couple to set a date. Many couples *did* get married under these circumstances, knowing the man was destined to report for duty but wanting him to have a wife back home to fight for. For all kinds of reasons, Jack couldn't see himself doing that. The fact that he was almost certainly going off to war, that he might return maimed or never return at all, that Elizabeth was a lovely young woman with a wonderful life ahead of her—these forces became for Jack something more than a wartime reality faced by so many. They became his excuse. Elizabeth wrote him a few letters once had he been sent into combat in the South Pacific. Jack never wrote her back.

The Tulane commencement ceremonies of 1943 were a two-step process for Jack. As is standard in college graduation, Jack heard his name called by the business school dean and walked across the stage in cap and gown to receive his diploma. Without even breaking stride, however, he moved on to the uniformed Navy commander to receive his commission as an ensign and his orders to fight the Japanese in World War II.

4

SHIPS AT SEA

WITHIN TWO DAYS OF HIS GRADUATION from Tulane, Jack caught a train from Union Station in New Orleans and headed north to the busy naval installation in the beautiful natural harbor of Newport, Rhode Island, where for generations America's wealthiest families had frolicked. He was to undergo several weeks of training before traveling to Quincy, Massachusetts, for the christening of his brand-new ship, the light cruiser USS Pasadena (CL-65). Then, after a bit more training and a shakedown cruise to the Caribbean, he was to help sail the ship through the Panama Canal, across the International Dateline and into the South Pacific. There, the forces of the Emperor of Japan were waiting.

Decades later, Jack remembers no particular drama surrounding his departure—yet after nearly three years of global warfare, America had probably grown accustomed to such partings. He said goodbye to his parents after the ceremonies in New Orleans. Later, places like Newport and Boston would become a regular part of his life, along with the people who inhabit them so gracefully. At this time, however, he was still a kid from Fort Necessity, Louisiana, who had seen little and done even less.

The *Pasadena* was what the Navy called a Cleveland-class light cruiser—thus her designation CL-65. She was essentially a weapon that moved across the waters, much more quickly than larger ships

Cruiser

Aboard the ship:
Jack 2nd from the left

like heavy cruisers, destroyers, battleships and, of course, the mammoth aircraft carriers that delivered the air war as American troops finally got the better of island after island and pushed up toward the mainland of Japan. Her main job, and what became Jack's job, was to shoot down enemy planes—the ones strafing, bombing and torpedoing US vessels from the sky or, with increasing Japanese desperation, slamming into ships on *kamikaze* suicide missions. The *Pasadena* and her fellow light cruisers also were outfitted with heavy artillery, which would be fired day and night onto islands like Iwo Jima and Okinawa to soften up Japanese defenses so the Americans could land with less chance of being slaughtered on the beach.

The *Pasadena* even had two planes of her own—seaplanes that could be launched from the deck with a massive lurch by catapult, check out Japanese ships and encampments by air and then return to a pontoon landing on the waves. They could then be lifted back aboard with a crane to await the next reconnaissance. Jack's ride in the seat behind the pilot of one such mission would prove one of his most exciting experiences in the entire war in the South Pacific.

The beginnings of this adventure of a lifetime sometimes felt like being back at Tulane. A good deal of the training at Newport, and later down in Norfolk, Virginia, involved sitting in a classroom taking notes. Still, as the weeks went on, theory found itself replaced with practice—with a vengeance. There was firefighting school in Brooklyn, which Jack hated, mostly because training involved crawling under real flames while pulling a heavy fire hose to douse the

The Navy: One of many hats worn by Jack

conflagration at its source. All this took place in the belly of a Navy ship. Not for the last time, Jack found himself fearing he'd never be able to get out of there alive.

What proved his most important training for the South Pacific took place at the huge naval installation in Norfolk. In gunnery, Jack shot at fast-moving planes like the ones he'd face in real life months later, or at targets pulled through the air behind real planes. Using 20mm guns, Jack and his compatriots would spend hours learning to

Ship life: Jack 2nd from center right, facing camera

gauge the speed of an aircraft and how to lead it with rapid fire, so it and the shells met up with a satisfying explosion in the air. "Your aim," as Jack simplifies the process so many decades later, "was to get the *kamikaze* before it got you."

The *Pasadena*'s crew made the quick trip across the state line to Bethlehem Steel's Fore River Shipyard in Quincy, Massachusetts, for their new ship's christening. The mayor of Pasadena, California, came to participate in the ceremony, and his wife performed the traditional honors of smashing a champagne bottle against the hull. In his remarks, Mayor C.G. Wopschall said his city was so proud of this ship that if it were sunk in the thick of the fighting, his constituents would pay to construct another. Jack remembers thinking that, as one of the guys who would probably die in such an occurrence, the mayor's words were not terribly reassuring. The *Pasadena*, which followed an earlier vessel used during World War I and preceded a submarine used in modern times, was officially commissioned for duty in the South Pacific on June 8, 1944—only two days after D-Day, the Allied

invasion of Normandy and the beginning of the end of the European war against Hitler's Germany and Mussolini's Europe.

Now man and ship could be one. Officially, the *Pasadena* was 610 feet long and 66 feet wide, weighed 10,000 tons and had a top speed of 32 knots—definitely not the tortoise in any race in open sea—and had a crew of Ensign Jack Grayson and 1318 other officers and enlisted men. On the weaponry side, the ship was armed with twelve 6-inch guns, another twelve 5-inch guns, plus twenty-eight 40mm guns and ten 20mm guns.

The ship's shakedown cruise took her to the island of Trinidad in the Caribbean, a time in which not only the weaponry but the vessel herself could be tested, and the men aboard could settle into the life that would be theirs for an indefinite period. While no day at sea during war is without fear, Jack remembers the cruise's scariest moments as sailing past Miami heading south and then heading back north. Even with wartime restrictions, the city was a bright line across the western horizon, and no one knew whether German U-boats were watching for the *Pasadena*'s silhouette with fingers ready to launch torpedoes. U-boats were spotted with regularity in the Atlantic along the Eastern Seaboard, making their way into the Caribbean and even through the Florida Keys into the warm Gulf of Mexico.

Returning from the shakedown cruise, but before setting out to join the war effort, Jack enjoyed a few pleasant weeks in Boston Harbor. There was still training and practice, now being carried out on Jack's ship with her own guns. During one noteworthy session in Boston Harbor, Jack and his men sighted their guns using the top of the Old North Church—famous for the Revolutionary War code about the redcoat advance: "One if by land, two if by sea." They had no intention of firing on the landmark, only of using its known coordinates to check the numbers they were getting from their equipment.

When not training, they indulged in a bit of upper-crust New England social life. Everybody, it seemed, loved the fighting man—or, in Jack's case, the soon-to-be-fighting man. Jack met people he

U.S.S. Pasadena

had only heard about, even during his time at Tulane among the old money of New Orleans. People wanted to meet him and to wish him well, people who had been in positions of social and business leadership not just for decades but, via their ancestors, for centuries. He met the governor of Massachusetts and enjoyed meeting the man's attractive daughter, although Jack didn't think it was time to begin anything romantic.

During his best night before leaving for war, he went to a bar in downtown Boston with his shipmates, meeting and finally pairing up with a group of girls who were there. Jack found himself with

Lois, from nearby Salem. And while he hid behind his now-practiced lines about going away to fight, not knowing what will happen and maybe dying young, he did work past his fear of rejection enough to ask Lois to write letters to him. She did this every single day for the remainder of the war.

Finally, it was time to sail. Jack said his goodbyes to Lois, right along with his promises to write. There was the long haul down to Panama first, since the canal across the isthmus was the quickest door to the Pacific Ocean. Again there was the boredom of shipboard life (the aspect of war that Jack believes filled more days than not) and again there were the tense hours passing before the lights of Florida and its fabled Gold Coast. The Panama Canal served up its series of levels and locks, with a peaceful cruise through Gatun Lake near the center, and the last piece of solid ground before the seemingly endless Pacific. It was here the *Pasadena* stopped for a while, not just for refueling but also for a mandatory visit (unofficially, unrecorded in the ship's log) to one of the largest bordellos on the face of the earth. It was called the House of Paradise.

The place, as Jack recalls, had hundreds of prostitutes ready and willing, surely some too old and others, technically, too young. There was alcohol to be guzzled and sex to be had; but once again Jack's shyness and embarrassment held him back, along with his equal fears of going to hell and catching one of the venereal diseases he had learned about from a Navy film. The best he could hope for is that none of his shipmates would notice. Ensign Jack Grayson departed the Americas and headed off into a fight that would cost ships full of young Americans their lives—still a virgin.

He did not, however, reach the South Pacific battle zone without any changes in his status. After stops in San Diego and then at Pearl Harbor in Hawaii, where the devastation left by the Japanese sneak attack of 1941 provide all the more incentive to fight, the *Pasadena* crossed the 180th Meridian, also known as the International Date Line. There was a time-honored ceremony to welcome each man who did so into the Order of the Golden Dragon. Jack was now a "trusted

dragonback," and forever after he would have the membership card to prove it.

From the day he sailed out of Pearl Harbor until the Japanese surrendered in Tokyo Bay after atomic bombs had wiped out Hiroshima and then Nagasaki, Jack was at sea—often beyond even the sight of land for days or weeks at a time. Still, there was a small atoll in the Caroline Islands that was the closest thing to something he and the rest of the men aboard the *Pasadena* could call home. The place was called Ulithi.

On September 23, 1944, a regiment of the US Army's 81st Division landed unopposed, followed a few days later by a battalion of Seabees. A survey ship examined the lagoon and found it capable of holding 700 vessels, more than either Majuro or Pearl Harbor—if only it could somehow become a port. The Navy transferred what islanders there were to another bump in the ocean called Fedarai and started filling Ulithi with what Admiral Nimitz called his "secret weapon," a group known to World War II history buffs as Service Squadron Ten. Within mere weeks, the Navy was able to create repair and re-supply facilities thousands of miles away from any actual Naval port. Pontoon piers of a new design were built at Ulithi, each consisting of four-by-twelve-foot pontoon sections, filled with sand and gravel, and then sunk. The pontoons were anchored in place by ropes to shore and by iron rods driven into the coral. Connecting tie pieces ran across the tops of the pontoons to hold them together into a pier.

The piers stood up incredibly well, despite extremely heavy weather. For Jack and the rest of the Navy, they would be lifesavers through the crucial sea Battle of the Leyte Gulf, the invasions of Iwo Jima and Okinawa and the brink of the much-feared land invasion of Japan.

As Jack was to discover happily at Ulithi, the Seabees weren't all work and no play. They also completed a fleet recreation center at Mog Mog Island that could accommodate 8000 enlisted men and 1000 officers every day, and they built a 1200-seat theatre, including a 25x40-foot stage with a Quonset hut roof completed in only twenty

days. At the same time, knowing what lay ahead for the US forces, the Seabees constructed a 500-seat chapel. What appeared to be a larger tanker distilled fresh water from the so-abundant saltwater and baked bread and pies. The fleet's all-important ice cream barge made 500 gallons each shift. By March 13, there were 647 ships at anchor at Ulithi. With the arrival of amphibious forces staging for the invasion of Okinawa, the number of ships at anchor peaked at 722. For seven months, the atoll was the largest and most active anchorage on the face of the earth.

Ulithi could be fun, Jack discovered. For one thing, beginning with his first experience of combat supporting the invasion of the Philippines and then bombarding the shores of Cam Ranh Bay (later famous in the Vietnam War), every day *not* fighting was a good day. And while Jack was never a big drinker, the fact that so many of his buddies knocked back plenty of beer and whiskey at Ulithi made for a lively time in the tropics. So many men fell into the water trying to climb up from the tenders that ferried them back to the *Pasadena* each night that a decision had to be made. After that, on each trip back to the ship, fifteen to twenty men were loaded into a cargo net and lifted by crane, like cargo in a port, onto the waiting deck.

Occasionally, the war did come to Ulithi, and its sunken legacies were reminders of the danger each time Jack and his shipmates returned from another mission. There was, for instance, the fleet oiler USS Mississinewa, sent to the bottom of the lagoon on November 20, 1944, by Japanese manned suicide torpedoes called *kaiten*. There was also a *kamikaze* attack on March 11, 1945, seriously damaging the aircraft carrier USS Randolph, which (it was later discovered) had left a cargo light on despite the nightly blackout.

Jack would remember that *kamikaze* attack in an extremely personal way. On that particular night, his *Pasadena* superiors had decided to show a movie on the deck, so they hauled out a huge screen and a clanking, old-style projector and started the film. It was *Laura*, Jack remembers, starring Dana Andrews and Gene Tierney. The men were totally absorbed in the story when the *Randolph* tied up right

next to them exploded into flames. Every man aboard the *Pasadena* scattered to his battle station, awaiting the next attack. But it never came. In fact, the plane that struck the *Randolph* had disintegrated on impact so completely that for a time no one knew what had happened. Since the fires had been put out, the men of the *Pasadena* slowly drifted back to the deck to finish watching the end of *Laura*.

5

INTO THE EMPIRE

TIME AND AGAIN, JACK'S SHIP HEADED OUT of the atoll to face combat, and time and again she was headed for a rendezvous with military history. The sailors seldom knew anything about their destination or their purpose, and at least as many days were spent at sea in boredom as in any form of terror. The men slept in steel bunks below the *Pasadena*'s waterline, each bunk with a mattress plus a special chemical cover that had to be spread over it when the sailor got up. The cover was designed to prevent fires, which could destroy the ship and every man on it. Jack and his compatriots were told that to forget the cover even once would mean a court martial. Even more dramatic was the night a Japanese shell hit the hull of the ship only inches from Jack as he slept. "If it had penetrated," he says calmly, "I wouldn't be here."

As a gunnery officer, Jack's battle station was a spot six decks down. Not only did he have to fight off *kamikazes* and other Japanese planes from a place where he couldn't actually see them but he also worried tirelessly about what would happen if their bombs hit home. In the interest of preserving the ship to fight again, Jack's position was sealed from the outside each time fighting broke out—"dogged down," the sailors called it—so that a rupture would fill only that section with rushing seawater. Jack and his shipmates spoke some-times about whether it would be less painful to suck in on purpose and drown quickly or to follow the water as it rose, gasping for air

until there was no more. "I changed my answer a lot," Jack says.

Essentially, Jack commanded all the *Pasadena*'s anti-aircraft guns by what amounted to remote control. Yes, there were sailors assigned to each gun, there to not only be eyes in the open air but to fire manually if the technology ever let the *Pasadena* down. Six decks below, Jack followed each Japanese plane as it swooped in fast and low, sometimes firing the 20mm and 40mm guns ahead of its angle and speed to destroy the enemy directly, other times exploding shells in the water in its path to bring it down. The latter technique was crucial to survival once Japanese pilots figured out they could fly in lower than the guns could be aimed. For the rest of his life, Jack would remember how it felt for his radar to give him solution, meaning the guns were locked onto an incoming enemy plane, and also how it felt to hear the reports from his guys up on deck. "No joy" meant he had missed the target. The word he wanted to hear was "splash."

The Battle of Leyte Gulf was a major turning point in the war against Japan: it opened the door to all the missions Jack and his shipmates would undertake, from the Philippines to Indochina and deep into the Japanese home islands. Before Leyte Gulf, each step northward across the map meant facing all or part of the empire's naval might. After Leyte Gulf, the emperor's naval forces never played a tide-turning role again.

The battle was that rarity in modern warfare: an old-fashioned sea battle of the sort that once destroyed the Spanish Armada and sent hundreds, perhaps thousands, of armed sailing ships to the bottom of the Mediterranean, the Atlantic and the Caribbean. This time it was mammoth aircraft carriers, battleships and destroyers being moved across the board, pounding and responding with the life-or-death energy of two boxers in a ring. Leyte Gulf proved a resounding victory for America's strategic commitment to "Carrier based naval warfare," in which the aircraft carriers brought US attack planes into range of each next target, always protected by a configuration of smaller, faster and more maneuverable ships. Commanded by Admiral William "Bull" Halsey, Task Force 38 within this overall

naval inventory came to include the *Pasadena*. After Leyte Gulf, the fighting for every inch of Japanese real estate would be bloody, sometimes even suicidal. But the sea battle flung open the door.

One the most terrifying things Jack experienced during the war was not the Japanese shells or *kamikazes* but a huge typhoon called Cobra. It happened on December 18, 1944, near Luzon in the Philippines. There were very clear warning signs on the radar of this impending monster storm of 120 mph winds coming straight at the US forces, but Halsey sailed directly into the typhoon's heart, reportedly saying "we're not a fair weather navy." The storm caused more damage to the US Navy than the Japanese ever did. People topside were washed overboard, three destroyers were capsized and sunk, hundreds of lives were lost, more than one hundred aircraft were wrecked or washed overboard, the decks on aircraft carriers were peeled upward and all ships suffered damage. On the *Pasadena*, several people were washed overboard and most of the guns were thrown out of alignment.

"Most all of us strapped ourselves into our chairs in the dining room," Jack remembers, "and once during the storm, I begged to go to the bridge, holding onto everything possible to watch each roll of the ship get closer and closer to coming to the 'righting moment,' past which it would capsize, and also waves of an estimated 100 feet high that buried half the ship when the bow went down, only to struggle up, shaking its head, only to bury itself again."

Later, a naval inquiry afterward found Admiral Halsey responsible for the losses of seven warships, untold damage to the ships and 1450 lives lost, more than the combined losses of the Battle of Midway and Battle of the Coral Sea. But the naval body took no action against him. Six months later he failed to steer his fleet clear of another typhoon.

In Jack's earliest battles, such as the ones for Luzon in the Philippines, for Formosa (today's Taiwan) or for Cam Ranh in Indochina, a deadly routine set in. For each assault, he took his station six decks down to fight off Japanese fighter planes while the

Pasadena's larger guns rained destruction on the shoreline. There was a belief—never entirely true and at Iwo Jima tragically untrue—that such bombardments left the Japanese with little ability or will to keep fighting.

Perhaps the matter was relative, with US soldiers and Marines hitting the beaches from their landing craft having an easier time than they would have had with no bombardment from their friends at sea. The retaking of the Philippines, while debatable in importance once Japanese troops were blockaded there and the sea lanes were clear, loomed large in at least one American commander's mind. It allowed General Douglas MacArthur to wade ashore and make good on the promise he made departing in 1942: "I shall return."

By February 1945, Jack Grayson was a battle-hardened veteran, not to mention an experienced man of the sea—during one sailing, in fact, the crew of the *Pasadena* went a full eighty days without touching dry land. This violent apprenticeship proved fortunate, because the worst was yet to come. "I'd never heard of the place," Jack says, remembering. "I had no idea what Iwo Jima even was."

In later years, some historians would argue that the scene of what was arguably the Pacific Theater's most famous battle didn't need to be fought at all. With hindsight, critics understood that Iwo Jima didn't play a significant role as staging area for future advances and that the cost in killed and wounded American soldiers was too high. Still, at the time, there was a two-month lull before the planned invasion of Okinawa, and Iwo Jima was expected to be a quick and relatively easy victory. With it and the other Japanese Volcano Islands pacified, the American forces would not have to keep looking over their shoulders as they moved ahead, wary of an attack from behind.

It was understood that the demeanor and approach of the Japanese fighting man had changed. Certainly Jack, spending day after day and night after night shooting down *kamikazes* intent on dying for the Rising Sun understood this. The war, most seemed to understand, was over and the Japanese had lost. What remained undecided was how many more months would have to pass and how many more

Americans would spill their blood to finish the job. Suicide attacks by Japanese fighters, in groups or individually, gradually became the nature of their defense—especially once their Navy had been neutralized in the Leyte Gulf and their remaining planes often lacked pilots trained in organized attacks. None of the planners, expecting Iwo Jima to surrender to the 60,000 US Marines and 450 warships in ten days or less, could know the Japanese side of such numbers. Of the 22,000 Japanese on Iwo Jima at the start of the battle, only 216 were ever taken prisoner—and most these had been wounded.

The *Pasadena* was part of the bombardment. At times it must have seemed a waste, since there were so few signs of civilization, or even of human life, on this island of dark volcanic ash. It was understood that the Japanese, however many of them remained, had dug into the earth in what amounted to bunkers and foxholes, but it wasn't until after the victory that Americans discovered the maze of tunnels that kept men and ammunition flowing freely from one station to another, even during the vicious bombing. When the US Marines went ashore in landing craft on February 19, Jack and his shipmates had good reason to hope that the attackers would have little left to do on Iwo Jima.

Jack's work was done when the bombardment was halted, so he made his way up those familiar six decks to the open air. As he watched with the aid of binoculars, the first waves of Marines encountered the last thing they were expecting—absolute silence. The beach began to fill with Marines, many units pushing cautiously into the rises just beyond. More Marines landed and looked around. Only when the beach was full of US forces did Jack see the volcanic ash blaze to life as Japanese fighters opened up from pillboxes and bunkers everywhere. Big guns atop Mount Suribachi rained shells down on the Americans, disappearing behind steel doors as soon as they had done their work. Contrary to first appearances, Iwo Jima was armed and dangerous. As the Marines took some of their heaviest casualties of the entire war, it quickly became clear that no one was about to give up.

Over the next four days, the Navy commanders were limited in how much they could do to help their compatriots locked in such desperate battle. At night, they still ordered the big guns to pound on Suribachi, since they knew that no US troops had reached that area yet. They also fired flares at night, to help the Marines see who or what was advancing. Many of the Japanese soldiers had by this point mastered enough unaccented English to call out to American troops by name; when the unlucky Marine stood up to answer, a burst of bullets sent him down. The scene was nightmarish, the heaps of volcanic ash strewn with bleeding bodies and even the deepest silence broken by the groans of wounded and dying.

By February 23, after almost constant hand-to-hand combat, the Marines reached the top of Suribachi, an achievement far more than symbolic. It meant that, often with the help of flamethrowers, the island's bunkers, pillboxes and tunnels had been cleared of the enemy. At great cost (American casualties exceeded Japanese), Iwo Jima was finally in American hands—though it would take weeks to kill the last Japanese die-hards. At some point on that day, Jack remembers getting an ice cream from the ship's mess hall and going up on deck. Gazing through his binoculars, he spotted a lone American flag waving high atop the dark, rocky mountain. He didn't pick out any soldiers, US or Japanese, standing around. Hours earlier, five Marines and one Navy corpsman had raised that flag as a young Associated Press photographer named Joe Rosenthal fired off frame after frame.

One of Rosenthal's exposures would take on a title, "Raising the Flag on Iwo Jima," and become iconic. It won the Pulitzer Prize, quickly graced a US stamp and, in 1954, served as model for the Marine Corps War Memorial by sculptor Felix de Weldon adjacent to Arlington National Cemetery.

Jack's final wartime rendezvous with destiny awaited him among the Ryukyu Islands of Okinawa. Sometimes referred to as the "typhoon of steel," the Battle of Okinawa, codenamed Operation Iceberg, would grind on from early April to mid-June and take its

place as the longest battle of the entire Pacific War. As Okinawa was only 340 miles from the Japanese mainland, it was considered essential to the planned (if dreaded) land invasion. And after fighting to virtually the last man on Iwo Jima, fears grew from the top commanders to the lowest enlisted man that the invasion of Japan would be drawn-out and bloody. The number one million was mentioned, projecting the possible loss of American fighting men as they moved from village to village, cave to cave. Okinawa would be mandatory to achieve such an invasion, as it would be close enough to launch air strikes on the mainland.

In fact, the Battle of Okinawa lasted so long that a historical moment took place during Jack's dangerous work there. On May 8, 1945, Adolph Hitler was found dead in his bunker in Berlin, and Germany surrendered to the Allies Forces unconditionally. Like all the US soldiers and sailors still fighting against Japan, Jack cheered the news. In addition to providing relief to any American, the German surrender also meant that military resources in Europe could be quickly diverted to the Pacific. Yes, Jack knew it was V-E (Victory Europe) Day in the United States and across Europe. But as the Japanese fought on to hold Okinawa, there was no time for a victory party. Only V-J Day could someday, somehow, allow the men of the *Pasadena* to celebrate.

The cost of taking Okinawa affected Jack in another way. Of all the bombardments he and his shipmates had handled since pressing outward from Ulithi in the Carolines what seemed a world away and a lifetime ago, Okinawa and its *kamikaze* attacks were truly devastating to the Navy. For once, the Navy's death toll was as high as that reported by the Army and the Marines. No fewer than twenty-seven vessels—twelve destroyers and fifteen amphibious craft—were sunk during the action. In all, 368 Navy vessels were damaged, including 120 of the amphibious boats used to land American troops on desolate beaches.

Of all the American deaths on land and at sea during the Battle of Okinawa, which proved to be the final official ground confrontation

of World War II, two were especially high profile. Lieutenant General Simon Bolivar Buckner Jr. was killed by enemy artillery while inspecting his troops, becoming the highest-ranking member of the US military to die in combat during the war. Also dying on Okinawa, the victim of a Japanese sniper, was beloved and Pulitzer Prize-winning war correspondent Ernie Pyle. After surviving the war across Europe and earning vast affection for depicting the regular GI, the dogface, the wearer of "The Thousand Yard Stare," Pyle had come to the Pacific because that's where the story now was. In Europe, with some dark irony, General George S. Patton had always preached that the only way for a warrior to die was by the last bullet of the last battle of the last war. On April 18, on the outlying island of Ie, Pyle the correspondent came closer to doing so than Patton the warrior did.

On August 6, the B-29 bomber *Enola Gay* of the 393rd Bombardment Squadron took off from the Pacific island of Tinian, its primary target an army depot and port called Hiroshima. The atomic bomb known as Little Boy detonated at 1750 feet above the ground, virtually flattening 4.7 square miles of the city, killing as many as 80,000 people and injuring 70,000 more. Three days later, when the emperor didn't surrender, the B-29 *Bockscar* lifted off from Tinian with a bomb called Fat Man. Cloud cover turned its secondary target into its primary, and Nagasaki entered the history books. Some 35,000 people perished in the swirling atomic blast, with 60,000 more injured. The emperor agreed to surrender.

"I cheered," Jack recalls of the moment he heard the news, the result of a secret that had been kept for years in a small laboratory in Los Alamos, New Mexico, and in the secret city of Oak Ridge, Tennessee. "It meant we wouldn't have to invade Japan. There was no way to know how many lives would have been lost had we done so. Really, we couldn't believe it. Nobody had thought about a bomb that big. And we didn't understand radiation at all."

Jack was aboard the *Pasadena* in Tokyo Harbor when representatives of the Empire signed the Japanese Instrument of Surrender and General MacArthur signed his acceptance on the deck of USS Missouri

U. S. S. PASADENA

Lieutenant (jg) Charles J. GRAYSON, USNR
was present in Tokyo Bay on 2 September 1945
at the signing of surrender terms of the Allied
Nations by the Japanese.

REAR ADMIRAL, U. S. NAVY
COMMANDER TASK FORCE 35

CAPTAIN, U. S. NAVY COMMANDER, U. S. NAVY
COMMANDING OFFICER EXECUTIVE OFFICER

The Japanese surrender: 1945

on September 2. One of dozens of US warships packing the harbor, Jack could see little of the ceremony through his binoculars and hear even less. He certainly couldn't see the American flag flying above the assembled officials: the one flown by Admiral Matthew Perry aboard USS Powhatan in 1853, when he opened long-mysterious and insular Japan to trade with the United States. He found the scene beautiful, both the natural curves of the harbor and the assembled might of his homeland. He also caught himself studying the big Japanese guns onshore, all the death and destruction he and his comrades in arms would have been forced to face had they invaded.

"We could see for miles and miles the utter devastation of Tokyo," Jack recalls. "It was flat—one hulk of a building standing in the distance, no power lines, no street signs, only a few people walking among the rubble, fifty-five-gallon drums with fires under them with boiling octopus inside for food. It was a total wasteland. Not a city."

To his credit, MacArthur treated the defeated Japanese with considerable respect that day aboard the *Missouri* and later throughout the occupation, forbidding US personnel to assault Japanese or to

eat any of their scarce food. Jack figured, though, that such rules had little to do with him. He was going home.

In the days that followed, many things became clear—not all of them happy. For one thing, the Japanese surrender did not quell resistance from lone-wolf fighters throughout the mainland and islands. Indeed, a few would still be fighting the war into the 1970s. All forays onto Japanese soil had to be matters of caution, and Jack always made sure he wore his officer's .45 pistol on his hip whenever he went ashore. And for another thing, his presumption of heading back to the States immediately—San Francisco, he assumed—turned out to be premature. Day after day, ship after ship sailed away, heading east into peacetime. Yet the *Pasadena* remained where she was anchored. Eventually, the news was shared: the admiral now assigned to the *Pasadena* was important to the occupation, so the ship would remain in Tokyo for an indefinite period. There were groans all around, but there was no court of appeal.

In an intriguing prelude to his later admiration for Japanese culture—and particularly for Japanese productivity on the job—Jack felt himself liking these people almost in spite of himself, and certainly in spite of years of wartime propaganda. In Tokyo at least, he experienced none of the hostility, resentment or bitterness that kept Americans carrying their weapons on the streets. He managed to arrange shore leaves with regularity, half a day here, even better two or three days there. And he traveled, ranging in destination between the devastation in and around Tokyo itself which he recalls as looking like it had been hit by a tornado, to Kyoto, the cultural and spiritual heart of Japan. As long as he lived, Jack would be grateful that those directing the firebombings and eventually the atomic bombs had turned away from destroying ever-graceful, ever-peaceful Kyoto.

The Japanese people behaved nothing like what Jack had been warned to expect. They were, in their own way, outgoing and friendly—many were openly apologetic about the terrible thing their leaders had led them into. They felt guilty, for the most part, and seemingly committed to making up to individual Americans what their

Kyoto: 1946, Jack at far right

Kyoto: 1946

empire had done to Americans as a nation. Men, women and children rushed out of their tattered homes whenever they saw Jack and his shipmates walking by, greeting them with bows and broken English, inviting them in for tea. By the end of a meandering shore-leave stroll, Jack and his comrades would be filled to the brim with hot tea. Many Japanese re-enacted their fears and sufferings under the American air bombardment, not with anger but with a request for forgiveness. "Bomb fall," Jack recounts an oft-repeated Japanese narrative. "Boom, boom, boom. Have some more tea."

Portrait of Jack Grayson by Benji Asada (1945)

During one of his visits to Kyoto, Jack met Japanese painter and printmaker Benji Asada, a rising star and later well respected artist in Japan. Fascinated with Jack and other US servicemen, Asada asked Jack to sit for a portrait. It would be the painter's first time to draw a Western face (a non-Asian face).

As a culmination of a long process, Jack made his way to a *geisha* house in Tokyo. He didn't know what to do there, but for once, he

knew exactly what he wanted. The geishas were undeniably beautiful, every one of them, yet Jack was drawn to one in particular. Her name, he determined, was Tesato—and with considerable trepidation, he inquired of the man in charge of the house how much it would cost to have sex with her.

"No, no," the man replied, hurrying to narrow the vast cultural divide. "*Geishas* are not prostitutes. You cannot simply pay to have sex with her. You must *buy* her. You must *marry* her. And her father must come to receive the money."

"I would like," Jack said, "to marry Tesato."

That, it turns out, is exactly what Jack did. In what seemed a timeless ceremony conducted entirely in Japanese, he became this *geisha's* "husband" and paid her father what he remembers as seventy dollars. He took her to a place nearby, a place filled with beauty as only the Japanese understand beauty, and lost his virginity. He knew so little about what to do, he realized, as he had again and again since his childhood spent in a world ruled by the Bible under the gaze of an angry, unforgiving God. The feeling of release, of acceptance, was so complete that Jack, decades later inadvertently quotes that same God on the day He first gazed out upon creation: "And it was good."

As the weeks passed, Jack and Tesato grew to love each other—she in her simple, open-hearted "You go ship, I come too" way, he in a manner that was always tentative, held in check by their time and place. They traveled through Tokyo and far beyond in an open Jeep that Jack could requisition. And she taught him, in many small lessons, not only about sex but about language and manners, about poise, about family. There were many things in this world that he didn't understand, and Tesato seemed to understand all of them.

Still, alone at night in his bunk aboard the *Pasadena*, Jack wondered what would happen when the inevitable came. But then they were together again, and none of it mattered. How could he do, really, what he wanted to do? How could he bring Tesato home to Fort Necessity? Introduce her to his country parents? Incorporate her into life on the farm, or indeed into any life in postwar America? None

of it made sense to him, and he spent many nights in sleepless, silent debate. In the end—six months after the Japanese surrender and three months after his ceremonial marriage to the *geisha* named Tesato—the *Pasadena* got its orders. Jack sailed out of Tokyo Harbor without saying goodbye. And he never attempted to contact Tesato again.

As a young man from the Louisiana countryside, he had no idea, as the ocean miles scrolled out between them, how operatic their story had been—or how much remorse he would carry with him always. "Sometimes I still wonder about her and feel sorry," Jack concedes.

6

PEACETIME

JACK INSISTS HE HAD NO CAREER GOALS, THAT
no ambitions bubbled to the surface as the *Pasadena* made its
way alone across the Pacific. Only months earlier, hundreds of
US ships had sailed home in convoys to a raucous hero's welcome.
That was all in the past, and virtually no one turned out to cheer Jack
and his shipmates as they sailed beneath the Golden Gate Bridge and
headed for a berth at Vallejo. America had, in the six months since
the Japanese surrender, gone back to work.

In retrospect, Jack's lack of career ambition was matched only
by his abundance of romantic ambition. His experiences with Tesato
had freed him from a great deal of the shyness that had quashed any
real experience with a woman before her. And certainly facing death
from the skies on a ship in a vast ocean had peeled back much of his
reticence. He knew there was Lois back in Salem, still writing him
long, affectionate letters, and thanks to a night at the iconic Fairmont
Hotel atop Nob Hill in San Francisco, there soon would be Margaret
as well.

Margaret was hardly a San Franciscan, however. She was a member
of the cast of the Rodgers and Hammerstein musical *Oklahoma*,
which was playing the city during the two months Jack spent there
waiting for his release from the Navy. She was based in New York,
where she had studied dance with the legendary Agnes de Mille, most
famous for creating the first ballet to appear in a Broadway musical,

in this case *Oklahoma*. One night Jack and his friends went into town and established themselves for a few hours at the Fairmont, including the Tonga Room that evoked so convincingly the South Pacific from which they'd just returned. As Jack remembers the night, Margaret was "pretty, bright, fun to talk to and lively." Within minutes, he was in love. Most importantly, even amidst Jack's first experience of being a "Stage Door Johnny," he promised to come visit Margaret in New York after the show closed in San Francisco. Having a semi-serious girlfriend in the Big Apple would help inspire Jack's later decision to attend the Wharton School of Business, only a brief train ride away in Philadelphia.

Eventually, the orders arrived and Jack was officially a civilian again. He could have hurried home to see his parents after his long stint in harm's way, or he could have raced in any direction on the compass to start a job that had been held for him—as many jobs were out of respect for America's men in uniform. Instead, Jack caught a slow, uncomfortable military transport plane to Boston, where it was easy to get to Salem and Lois.

By all accounts, both his and later hers—Lois phoned Jack decades later after surviving two husbands, only a year or so before she herself passed away—they had a wonderful time together. But he didn't marry Lois.

It's hard to say exactly what caused Jack's marital reticence, especially as servicemen took vows in droves all around him and nine months later started the Baby Boom. At first it had been the uncertainties of a world at war. Now there was the uncertainty of having no job, no income to support the family that was almost sure to follow. Jack seemed to be waiting for something. Yet he also seemed the last person capable of guessing what that might be.

From his base in Fort Necessity, the unemployed and largely unoccupied Jack tracked down his friend Charles Scott from the *Pasadena*. Scott, from Jackson, Mississippi, had "made a fortune" off his buddies playing poker on the ship. Now Jack said to him, "Let's go take a trip around the country." Only a few years before

Jack Kerouac would turn such a journey into American mythology, Jack and Charles bought an old Packard that needed fresh oil every 200 miles and drove north to Chicago, east to New York and finally down the East Coast by way of Atlanta. Jack would see no reason to visit Georgia Military Academy, since a real war had replaced all the pretending he had endured there.

Having managed to convince Lois he was simply not marriage material, Jack felt free to pursue whatever career dreams he could identify—and reignite his relationship with Margaret in New York. By the time he settled on attending Wharton in the fall of 1946, weekends in New York City would become Jack's habit.

Wharton was the oldest business school in America, second only to Harvard Business School in terms of overall prestige. Even without any specific career goals, Jack figured that whatever he attempted to do with his life would involve business and that an MBA would be helpful. There was also, he admits, the GI Bill, which was sending so many veterans to college in the first few years after the war. Jack had earned credit in that big government ledger, and he was committed to getting and spending his share.

Completely to his surprise, "business" wasn't a specific enough major for his one-year MBA program. When asked what he'd be majoring in, his answer was classic Jack Grayson: "I don't know." Since the advisers could see he'd taken several accounting classes at Tulane (only to avoid early morning class start times), they suggested he major in that discipline with an eye toward earning his CPA. While he never did practice as a CPA, Jack did earn his CPA certification while he was teaching his first year at Tulane.

For several months at the beginning of his studies at Wharton, it appeared once again that Jack had a serious girlfriend. He certainly caught the train to New York often enough and had a wonderful time in the city. There was Margaret, of course, loving him and offering increasingly frequent suggestions of matrimony. There were frequent trips to the theater—Margaret knew how to pull strings and get great seats—along with Jack's earliest extended encounter with

ballet and opera.

These New York weekends also marked Jack's first awareness of gay men, common in and around the theater but nonexistent or hopelessly closeted among the austere Methodists of Fort Necessity. He found them an entertaining addition to a new world that was light, clever and always fun. Eventually, as Margaret's gentle prodding toward the altar and her parents' firmer insistence proved stifling, Jack pulled away. He would miss New York as much as he would miss her. Decades later, though, he would still be showing off newspaper clippings about Margaret's success in *Oklahoma* in San Francisco, a beautiful city, filled with memories, built on foundations set down by his Grayson ancestor and perched on the Pacific for which Jack himself fought.

Wharton's Man of the Year: Jack in center

Jack earned his MBA from the same institution that counts Warren Buffett of Berkshire Hathaway, William Paley of CBS, Donald Trump of the Trump Organization and John Sculley of Apple among its success stories, as well as Justice William Brennan of the US Supreme Court. Founders and CEOs have always abounded in each year's graduating class, along with less notable graduates as well. Jack would find himself back on the campus decades later to receive Wharton's "Man of the Year" award in 1973 in recognition for his work to help the economy.

Among the MBA hopefuls at Wharton, there was no shortage of talk about future plans. Jack doesn't remember having any, but one thing was certain: his future plans did not include the farm in Fort Necessity. Presumably its continued existence formed a reassuring

corner of stability at the back of his mind, but all of his visions for the next step involved big cities and, increasingly, some sort of acquaintance with Europe. Even as he studied how to break into the American business universe, he was planning to break out somehow.

As expected, Jack disliked all his accounting and tax courses. They were so dry. Searching for some creative outlet, some vague artistic expression he could not begin to identify, Jack failed to note that deciding which column to put which number in was perhaps the most creative aspect of business.

As often in these postwar years, Jack's attention was elsewhere. He had fallen in love with an undergraduate named Ruth, and he spent much of his free time going with her to visit her parents just north of Philadelphia's Belt Line. Thus emerged a new rendition of Jack's now-standard double life: weekdays at the Delta Tau Delta house near Wharton (where he was allowed to rent a room after belonging to the fraternity at Tulane) and weekends among the swells in what would later become known as John O'Hara Country.

Jack remembers his love of opera reaching new heights with Ruth, both at the opera house and also at an Italian restaurant that played old Caruso records when the waiters themselves weren't hitting the high Cs. With Ruth on his arm, he came to love Philadelphia, its great museums (much later in life, he would follow the path of Rocky Balboa up those famous steps), its beautiful old buildings, its exotically ethnic neighborhoods. Eventually, though, Ruth's parents convinced her she should demand an engagement ring or break things off. No ring proved forthcoming.

To earn his MBA, Jack was required to research and write a thesis. His choice of topic is fascinating, even seen through the lens of his later years and accomplishments. Jack chose to assess the Tennessee Valley Authority (TVA), which had come of age as a way of creating jobs during President Franklin D. Roosevelt's Works Progress Administration program. The TVA, in addition to any economic impact, ended up changing the face of the South with dams, lakes and hydroelectric power. The TVA had, at the time, claimed to create a

yardstick by which to measure the efficiency of private power companies in order to rule on their rate requests. After considerable study and at least some thought, Jack decided this yardstick had no validity, since it failed to account for the TVA's use of dams to control flooding and encourage waterway navigation. In other words, the billions spent on the project wasn't just for power, so any efforts to balance cost with benefit was doomed to be nonsense. Best of all, Jack recalls, the thesis got him his MBA.

The New Orleans to which Jack chose to return—"It seemed like a good place to go," he says simply—is, sadly for its many admirers, only a memory of itself now. At that time, however, the city remained, even after so many of its sons and daughters had traveled during the war, a lost world of old families, old traditions and old money. It was still the Queen of the South, still the place in which to keep a townhouse if you owned a sugar or cotton plantation along its storied River Road on the Mississippi. In business terms, New Orleans still outranked brash, cultureless upstarts of the New South like Atlanta to the east and Houston to the west. And in terms of its port, it still out-hustled and out-handled newcomers like Mobile and Galveston. If you wanted to do business with Latin America and, by association, the rest of the world, the business you did still was likely to pass through New Orleans, largely unchanged in 1947 from what Thomas Jefferson would have seen when he made the Louisiana Purchase.

Jack tracked down his old Tulane friend Nigel, only to learn that he was planning on law school. Jack didn't want to be a lawyer. He also didn't want to teach—presumably to teach anything to anybody. But when he heard about an opportunity to become an instructor at his New Orleans alma mater, Jack actually applied for a job for the first time in his life. And got it. Ironically, this meant that Jack Grayson was now a teacher of accounting, a subject he hated.

Between knowing Nigel and being associated with Tulane, Jack spent the first two years of his professional life becoming enmeshed in the seasonal and social life of New Orleans. Both these points of entry

suggested the sublime and sedate world of Uptown New Orleans, but Jack certainly made his way into the raucous French Quarter numberless times as well. He learned about the arcane call out system used to escort young ladies to their masked dates at Mardi Gras balls, about the highly political debutante hierarchy, about the night parades that still, in those days, passed through real New Orleans neighborhoods suggested by their names (Freret, Carrollton, etc.) rather than along a single, better-secured route. He learned about the beginning of Carnival season, Twelfth Night with its tradition of king cakes and also about its end—the meeting of the courts of Rex and Comus at the Municipal Auditorium. Many lifelong New Orleanians would never see such blue-blooded ceremonies in person, but Jack did. His understanding of New Orleans deepened with every encounter.

From time to time, Jack's parents came down from Fort Necessity to visit. He always convinced them to stay at The Roosevelt Hotel, which had come into its own via the patronage of Governor Huey Long in the late twenties and early thirties under its charismatic owner, Kingfish crony Seymour Weiss. Staying at The Roosevelt invariably meant sampling Huey's favorite drinks in the bar, the Sazerac and the Ramos Gin Fizz—both of which Long had trumpeted to the nation when he went to Washington as a senator. Jack loved that his parents' visits always included these cocktails for his girlfriends, and especially that they always picked up the tab.

After two years of teaching accounting at Tulane, however, Jack decided he'd had enough of academia—perhaps forever, but certainly for now. In a conviction that would guide so much of his own work as an academic later, Jack decided it wasn't enough to teach. It was important to get out there and actually do something. Many could and would disagree with his unflattering assessment of academic life, but he would never entirely change it or leave it behind. At some point—he doesn't recall if the conversation occurred over the telephone or while watching the bartender at The Roosevelt spin a glass in the air with anisette to make another Sazerac—Jack said to Nigel, "Let's go to Europe."

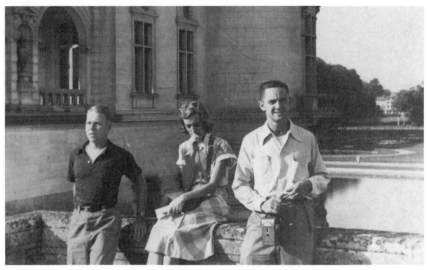

Jack (right) in Europe with Nigel (left)

As it had been for several previous generations of young Americans, Paris was shorthand for Western Europe. Since the time of the Grand Tour that always attracted the New World aristocracy to the heart of the Old World and continuing through generations of American artists and writers who wanted their dollars to last longer in a setting free from Puritanism, Paris equaled liberation. The fact that Paris itself had been liberated so recently added a sense of earned ownership to its already-heady allure. Paris was where you went if you were an American, if you knew what you wanted to do with your life—and even if you had no idea. You could live there on practically no money until you figured it all out.

Jack and Nigel made their way to Pensacola on the Florida Gulf Coast and found a French freighter loaded with peanuts bound for Europe. They had only $1200 between them, but the fare to take one of the four compartments not filled with peanuts was exceedingly low. The freighter made its way out of the Gulf around the tip of Florida and angled upward toward the north Atlantic. It wasn't long before a storm struck the ship with a vengeance and Jack Grayson, late of the *Pasadena* and a few thousand miles of the Pacific, got the

worst case of seasickness of his life. He remembers crawling up and out onto the deck and wishing he could die.

Far out at sea, however, a vision presented itself. RMS Queen Mary steamed across the freighter's path, sailing from Southampton to New York with all her many comforts. She was slicing through the waves rather than riding them up and down, and Jack swore to himself he was never coming home unless he could do so aboard the *Queen Mary*. When he found himself on solid ground, one of the first things Jack did was purchase a ticket to America on the *Queen Mary*, for use anytime during the next year.

Jack and Nigel disembarked at Dunkirk in France in a small lifeboat, knowing full well the story of how the British Army was saved from the Nazis early in the war by every last vessel that could be rounded up ferrying men to England across the channel. The Miracle at Dunkirk, it was often called, and it certainly preserved England long enough for Churchill to convince Roosevelt to join the war. Paying only a quick tribute, however, the two young men caught a train to the City of Light.

They spent only a handful of days in Paris seeing the most basic sights, from the Champs-Elysées to the Eiffel Tower and the *Folies Bergère*. Then they headed across the channel to London, attracted by free lodging at a home Nigel's family had outside the city. A child of the New World, whose main travels to date were to places built the night before by Seabees, Jack marveled at the ancient buildings of England surrounded by carefully manicured gardens. He had heard of "English gardens," and now he saw why they were notable. Living for virtually nothing with Nigel's family, the two were free to concentrate their financial resources on meeting girls. In England, and indeed for the rest of their tour, they started taking turns telling sweet young things touring the Continent that it was one of their birthdays. The young lady in question would turn to her parents, who were invariably nearby, and suggest they take the birthday boy and his friend out to dinner. This ruse got them female companionship, along with any number of free meals.

After London, Jack and Nigel's Grand Tour began in earnest. They crossed the English Channel back to Belgium, bought a used Peugot in Paris and then drove north to the near-mythical countries of Scandinavia—which had been liberated from the Nazis with a minimum of devastation. The big battles, in other words, were fought farther south. The young men drove through Denmark, where Jack remembers the Little Mermaid statue in the Tivoli Gardens and Hamlet's brooding castle with a terrific Swedish massage right next door; Sweden and Norway; then south to Amsterdam, where a tasting tour of the Heineken brewery was a major highlight. Considering the enormity of the struggle so recently concluded, Jack and Nigel entered Germany not sure what to expect. Surely Jack pondered the similarities between the welcome afforded them by everyday Germans and that given the *Pasadena* crew by everyday Japanese. History would judge the Allies to be victors in the conflict against Germany, yet as early as 1947 Americans were often made to feel like liberators.

"One minute you're trying to kill each other," Jack recalls thinking, "and the next minute you're all locking arms and singing." While in Bavaria, Jack picked up a German saying he would translate in later years to instruct his business students: "All your skill is in vain if an angel pisses on your flintlock." In others words, there's a large serving of sheer luck involved in any business success.

For a final few months before settling into daily life in Paris, Jack and Nigel toured the Mediterranean world, starting with the Italian culture capitals of Venice, Florence and Rome. Neither man seemed to have a better than rudimentary understanding of the cultures they were strolling through, except to note that so much of their legacy had been reduced to rubble by the war. The Marshall Plan of American aid had not yet begun to rebuild the glories of the past, an investment in a New Europe that would make it the first destination of airplane-based "mass tourism" little more than a decade later. As though checking sights off a list, the two visited the graceful, gifted island of Capri off the coast of bombed-out Naples, then headed back north to gaze at

the Leaning Tower in Pisa. Having entered Italy via the Swiss Alps, they decided to leave it via the blue sea at Monte Carlo.

Arriving in Paris, Jack and Nigel began a mostly open-ended (other than Jack's ticket for the *Queen Mary*) stay, cajoling girls for birthday dinners and taking temporary jobs as dishwashers or construction workers. The Continent was still in such disarray that doing such things was easy, without the permit and visa restrictions set in place later. Echoing many writers—but none more than his literary hero of the time, Ernest Hemingway, writing wistfully as an old man—Paris proved that promised moveable feast. And like Hemingway, Jack would carry its young-man joys and sorrows as memories for the rest of his life. "We had not much money, but no timetable," Jack says. "It was one of my freest and finest years."

By this point, Jack had tired of churches and museums, the sites all Grand Tours live and breathe. He simply wanted to be. That meant long solo walks along the Seine, punctuated by operas at the Opéra-Comique, best of all when some American girl's parents were paying for the ticket. At some point, Jack conjured the image of Hemingway crafting one painful, disciplined sentence at a time at a café table with a glass of Dubonnet at his elbow. Jack wasn't totally sure how to craft the sentences, and especially not how to make them his and not Hemingway's, but in cheap postwar Paris on the Left Bank the café table and Dubonnet could be arranged.

By all accounts, Jack missed the Hemingway lecture about "write what you know." The first story he tried to write was about a voodoo queen back in New Orleans—he knew nothing about voodoo. He also attempted a short story describing a woman's feelings while being raped. He had no expertise there either. He did not preserve these early efforts at fiction, considering them junk, then and now. His judgment shows all signs of being correct.

The vision of Jack writing like Hemingway in Paris, sentence after sentence on individual sheets of unlined paper, is noteworthy. It was the first vision of an actual career Jack ever seriously entertained. Then again, his serious pursuit of this dream kicked in only when

there were no pretty young farm girls from Provence living in the apartment that he and Nigel rented. And eventually, having started the clock himself by buying that ticket, the clock simply ran out. Jack, who traveled to the Old World aboard a now-forgotten freighter loaded with peanuts, traveled home to America and the rest of his life aboard the *Queen Mary*, one of the most famous ocean liners of all time. Nigel stayed on in London for a period and then returned to New Orleans as well.

Despite tossing out his attempts at fiction from this adventure, Jack did hold onto one example of his early nonfiction—a diary in a burgundy and gold leather binding that over the intervening years has begun to fall apart. Mostly the day-to-day notations of an American touring the Continent (each entry dated French-style, as in *10 Juin 1949*), the booklet does have flourishes and insights. One early passage, for example, serves up equal parts young writer trying to find his voice and young man trying to find himself.

"Awoke this morning to rattles of doorknob, shriek of wind, gray skies, hiss of water," Jack wrote in careful, slanted penmanship as the ship began to head into open ocean off Cape Hatteras.

"Long swells began to break under winds that topped the uneven tops with white frosting. Rain dotted the surface like holes in pancakes, and the ship was buffeted under blows from wave and wind... Read Arthur Miller's *Death of a Salesman* and was exceptionally impressed. It seems that one of the characters has something in common with me, no knowledge of what he wants out of life or what job he wants. His was resolved but was of no help to me."

7

NEWSPAPERMAN

"**I** HAD LEFT FOR EUROPE FROM NEW ORLEANS, so it was only natural that I would return there," Jack says, giving more credit than necessary to the time he'd spent in the city so far. He was still tagging along with Nigel, who "had the contacts and had the convertible," which surely eased his way back into his old New Orleans life as he moved toward a new one. Besides, after the years he had spent in the South Pacific, followed so closely by Wharton and then by Europe, it probably felt good to list someplace as "residence," even when it was a bit of a stretch.

Back in New Orleans with no money, no published works and no desire to go back to the farm, Jack decided first he had to try to continue to write stories and hope for the best. He wanted to find a place to continue attempting to write and found one with Nigel's help. Fannie Campbell ran a well-known boarding house in the Garden District. It was at the intersection of Prytania and Harmony, consisting of two columned houses adjoining one another that held about forty people, with an open backyard for parties at odd times.

Jack, Nigel and a new friend Jim Garrison, who was a fellow law student with Nigel at Tulane, took up residence in one of the boarding houses. Besides his writing attempts and standard revelry, Jack also found himself schooled in the world of law as he was often enlisted to help Jim prepare for moot court cases. Jim would later become New Orleans district attorney and convince

ilmmaker Oliver Stone that the CIA was behind the Kennedy assassination.

Fannie had a socially connected background but didn't like the correct and stuffy behavior of much of old New Orleans. Her only requirement to be a paying boarder in her two houses was that you liked to have fun, especially after dinner where she often strummed a homemade washtub base in her playroom or had a dance on the patio. She served a seated dinner each night at about seven tables. All men wore jackets but no ties, and women came (some former queens of well-known Mardi Gras balls) dressed for dinner and often half-drunk from afternoon gin parties. There was a lively discussion each evening that Jack should have written about, but didn't. When the Mardi Gras Rex parade came by on St. Charles at Mardi Gras each year, Fannie would enjoy a ride of her own right afterward—on an impromptu float pulled by two old mules, with the lady herself sitting on a toilet bowl and waving a plunger as her scepter.

All this came to an end when Fannie decided to sell her houses, and the Three Musketeers moved out to find individual accommodations. Jack chose the French Quarter in a tiny "slave quarter" near Bourbon and St. Louis overlooking a courtyard behind a gate. Jim went to an apartment opposite the famous restaurant Antoine's. And Nigel moved to a house in the Garden District.

Jay Teasdel was another close friend during these days, often playing chess with the friends at the Napoleon House bar. Coming from a moneyed family, Jay showed his independent spirit by buying a Rolls Royce and driving his friends around in it, flying to Honduras to have a made-to-order sailing boat built for him with a library and a fireplace and owning several apartments in the French Quarter right across from Brennan's restaurant. As adventurous as Jack, Jay has walked the world and written books about the experiences. At the time of this writing, Jay is still going strong, and he and Jack remain in touch.

In between frequenting jazz bars, drinking Hurricanes at Pat O'Briens, playing chess at the Napoleon House with Jim, Jay and

Typical gathering at Fannie Campbell's boarding house in New Orleans

Nigel, delighting debutantes at Mardi Gras time and befriending strippers, Jack continued to write about things he knew nothing about. He came to realize, at last, that he simply was not going to come near being a Hemingway. He worked through his options. The one that sounded best was to drag whatever passed for his writing talent down to Newspaper Row—down to *The New Orleans Item* specifically, since he liked its spunky style and focus on scandals that sold papers—and talk somebody into hiring him. In those days, the editors-in-chief of daily newspapers didn't live protected lives, which explained how many of them ended up with bullet wound scars. Jack was able to stroll past the glass-encased bulletin boards that displayed the *Item*'s main pages to the outside world, pass beneath the raised steel fire escape and enter the four-story, fast-paced, big-windowed, clicking-clanking-dinging world at 722 Union Street, the domain of the *Item* editor Clayton Fritchey.

Fritchey took the time to chat with the young man, asking him about his background and his goals. He was surely impressed with Jack's education at Tulane and Wharton, on the assumption that few in his newsroom had completed more than a year or two of college.

Eventually, Fritchey called over the city editor and said, "This guy wants to come work here." Turning to Jack, he completed the most important thought: "We pay practically nothing."

"I'll take it," Jack said.

Like many reporters before him, and some for a decade or two after, Jack can't recall his time at the *Item* without referencing *The Front Page*. Set in Chicago, the play that inspired at least two Hollywood films is one long love poem to journalistic adrenalin and savvy operators in rumpled suits. Jack was assigned to the City Room, where all the local news was gathered and (in the jargon of a later era) "packaged" for the new edition. And since the *Item* was an afternoon daily—even more, an afternoon daily with competition—that meant coming into work at five or six in the morning, grabbing assignments and then pounding the pavement for stories. Whenever Jack was assigned a photographer, he noticed tendency of the breed to stop at a café on the way and knock back a coffee laced with no small amount of bourbon. After working his beats, which would change over a couple of months or so, it was time to grab a cab back to the paper and pound out copy in time for the 10 a.m. and noon deadlines.

The production schedule of an afternoon paper like the *Item* defined what it did and how it did it. By comparison, slower-moving creatures like the morning *Times-Picayune* gathered news all day long, wrote it or sat on it till late at night, occasionally even pondering its importance before deciding where (if anywhere) to run it. At an afternoon paper, there was no such luxury of time. Stories were written and printed in early editions with the barest of details and sometimes even barer confirmations. By the time that day's final edition was on the press, many a front-page banner headline had petered to become a brief in the back. Every second was urgent—even when it turned out not to be.

In the iconic newspaper tradition, Jack was first put to work writing obituaries of the people who had died, calling the family for biographical details and calling the funeral home or, this being New Orleans, the Catholic Church, for arrangements. The young man did

well enough to be promoted—to writing obits of people who hadn't died yet. This made sense, of course, since it meant the bulk of the story would be ready when word came of a prominent death. Jack remembers realizing, even in these early stages at the *Item*, that what really sells newspapers is bad news. Good news, he decided, was boring.

His fellow reporters at the *Item* were fun. He went around with (and eventually dated) the paper's fashion editor Betty Jane Holder, thus breaking out of the boys' club that newspapers of an earlier era tended to be. In general, after handling all the jobs with skill and spirit while the men were off at war, the women reporters had contracted back into the "women's page," where big stories might be a wedding or the latest crop of New Orleans debutantes. During his year with the paper, in fact, many of Jack's dates were with women who worked with him at the *Item*.

Jack's first beat was the civil courts. He found the lawsuits and divorces to be boring. The sameness was enough to make Jack wish for assignment to the criminal courts, which is where he found himself after a couple of months. Early each morning he'd go to the white-marble monstrosity across from Brennan's in the French Quarter and check out who was being held. Prisoners shouted at him from behind bars, cursed him as though he had arrested them, as he looked over the paperwork in search of a story. It was, arguably, a natural step from the criminal courts to Charity Hospital, where the victims of crimes and terrible accidents tended to end up. Jack spent much of his workday waiting by the entrance to the emergency room, watching people come in or be carted in with snakebites, gunshot wounds or labor pains. He saw one man walk in under his own power and show the doctors a knife protruding from his side. Jack also noted the number of men injured in accidents while with their mistresses, men who begged him not to put their names together in the paper.

There were no excuses. Jack heard over and over from the co-workers who formed his apprenticeship on the fly, "You have to get the story." One morning a news tip came in that a small boy had drowned while swimming at Audubon Park. Jack took the

information and headed for the boy's home to get more. When the door opened, he asked awkwardly if the home was the residence of this young man. "Oh yes," the parents responded. "But he's not here right now. He's swimming at Audubon Park." Though it pains him to this day, Jack felt compelled to tell the couple their son was dead. "They screamed when I told them, and it tore me up," he recalls. "Before I left I asked could I have a picture. And you know, that was the first thing the editor asked for when I got back."

The police beat was next, and certainly there is no beat in journalism more colorful. All reporters both love and hate cops, and most of all they feel like they are cops—a natural result not only of constant proximity but also of working nights, weekends and holidays. The police beat in those days belonged to a reporter for the *States*, a competing newspaper, named Jack Dempsey, with the same name as the heavyweight champ but no blood relation, who coddled his police sources by bringing them donuts every single morning. There was probably room for only so many donuts, even at a police station, but the *Item*'s top police reporter was no slouch either. Benjamin Franklyn Hay had sources within sources, each cajoled, threatened or bribed to call him before they called Dempsey. Jack learned that part of the trick, when calling in a story, was to load in as many officers' names as humanly possible. Most police stories, therefore, featured only one bad guy and many boys in blue.

Slowly earning his editors' trust, Jack was given a wider field to roam, sometimes with memorable experiences, if not always grand results. He was asked to do an interview with Leander Perez, the boss of nearby Plaquemines Parish who had already stood up to Huey Long and would later defy the federal government over integration. As Perez wouldn't grant an interview, Jack talked to dozens of people about him, wrote his story and turned it in. His editor said it was fine: Now go show it to Perez at his New Orleans office and ask him for a comment. "The Judge," as Perez was invariably known, still refused to speak on the record, but then added a dark postscript. "I don't want the story," Perez snarled, jabbing his cigar toward Jack.

"I want you to get the hell out of my office. And remember: your name is now in my black book." Thankfully, Jack was never pulled over for speeding down near Pointe à la Hache.

Another, similar assignment sent him to profile Mob boss Carlos Marcello, who controlled vice not only around New Orleans but all the way to Galveston, Texas, and up to Dallas, where his associate Jack Ruby would kill the man who killed President Kennedy. Marcello wouldn't talk to the press, of course, and Jack couldn't get anyone to open the gate in the wall that surrounded his mansion. So Jack, remembering a piece of his mentor's advice—"You just don't give up. You do anything it takes."—climbed painstakingly over the wall and dropped down onto the lawn. Two large and snarling dogs came surging in his direction, making the wall remarkably easy to clear while escaping.

From the start of his time as a newspaperman, Jack managed to create stories his editors then asked or allowed him to write—in the trade, these are logically called "enterprise stories," and Jack had no shortage of that quality. His first were the three columns he wrote about his then-recent travels in Europe, under the standing headline "Travel and Travelers." Not exactly destination pieces *oohing* or *ah-hing* about the sights, these were both more conversational and more journalistic. In the column called "How Is It in Europe, in General, I Mean?" Jack talks about the physical legacy of the war years. "France hasn't been able to clean up as well in the smaller cities," he says. "Many gutted buildings still stand; and villages, particularly in the landing area, look ghostly when you realize what was once there."

Also dropping into Jack's lap was a regular column of business news called "Brokers and Bankers." The regular business reporter quit one day and the bosses, looking around the City Room, remembered they had an MBA from Wharton sitting there. So the column became Jack's—mostly short notes on local success or failure or local reaction to national business stories or sometimes nothing much at all. While he used words like "street gossip" a lot, he insists now he made up a lot of things just keeping an eye on the stock market and beyond. The

subheads within a typical "Brokers and Bankers" column say it all: Visit Markets, Canadian Here, Plan Convention, Parish Issue Sold, Meeting Postponed, Bulls Happy and Wesson Statement.

Arguably, Jack's biggest story at the *Item* ("Lives Here, But... He Bid $160,000!") concerned an elaborate scam in neighboring Jefferson Parish to buy up bonds under a false name before a bond election would generate huge profits. As befits an afternoon daily, much was made of the *Item* discovering this malfeasance and sending Jack to Jefferson to track down the "carpenter mystery man" being used as a front. As happens with many such scandals, the bond issue passed, the secret owners of the bonds made their profit and nobody cared about it ever again.

When he wasn't working his specific beats, or generating his impressing string of enterprise stories, Jack went wherever he was sent. His bound volume of clips from the *Item* include interviews with inventor Rube Goldberg, with the 1950 Maid of Cotton and with British fashion designer Norman Goldson ("Plaids on Way Back"), overviews of the Mid-South's railway system with New Orleans as its terminus and a series of sentimental Christmas stories about local citizens down on their luck that was still continuing to solicit donations decades after Jack left the paper.

Jack's personal life included not only dates with coworkers and adventures with the social set (arranged by Nigel) but fairly regular visits by Jack's parents. As in his time at Tulane, it apparently didn't take much to inspire them to visit—still staying at The Roosevelt, still having drinks in the Sazerac Bar. Jack introduced them to some of the young women he was squiring around, even took seven or eight up to see the farm, but none of those relationships proved to be serious. He always knew the girls his mother would like and the ones she wouldn't, and it became kind of a game to predict her reactions. He never had to tell his parents, at least until later, "Mom, Dad, this is the woman I'm going to marry."

A wedding Jack attended as a groomsman changed the course of his life, even though he never intended to remain at the *Item* or

indeed work for newspapers his entire career. Perhaps he was trying to follow Hemingway's advice to work as a reporter but not for "too long." At any rate, as he and his fellows were helping the groom get ready for the ceremony, Jack noticed something lying on the hotel bed. There was a badge, and there was a gun. He knew his friend had recently completed the FBI Academy in Quantico, Virginia, but he had never given the FBI much thought. Now, it resonated with him. Like the groom, he had a wedding to get through, but the vision of the badge and gun stuck with him, even day after day as he wrote his stories for the *Item*.

Preliminary inquiries led him to the FBI office in New Orleans and a conversation with the SAC, as the ornate FBI parlance adopted by director J. Edgar Hoover referred to the Special Agent in Charge. The SAC gave Jack a hypothetical set of circumstances and then called in a secretary to type up the report he dictated, little realizing that Jack probably typed better and faster than anybody in the room. "Thank you very much, we'll be in touch," was the dismissal. Yet it proved to be more than that. Weeks later Jack was informed that he'd been accepted into the FBI Academy. He too might become a special agent, a G-Man, a J. Edgar Hoover. He too might get a badge and a gun.

Clayton Fritchey, his editor and mentor who would later become an aide to President Harry Truman, was sorry to see Jack go. He felt Jack had a bright future as a journalist, even if the prospect of making "practically nothing" remained a truism of newspaper life. As he gathered the few pieces of his life-to-date around him for the trip to Quantico, Jack reflected on what he had learned.

He had spent a year chasing politicians and prostitutes, celebrities and scam artists, several Bourbon Street strippers like the Cat Girl and Blaze Starr (who would make headlines a few years later as the girlfriend of Governor Earl Long, Huey's brother) and no small number of rapists and murderers. The *Item* had given him what he came to call a "slice of life," the chance for a young man still naïve in so many ways not just to feel grownup but to be grownup. And to realize, as all grownups must, that things are seldom what they seem.

"I learned about people, and I learned about deadlines," Jack says. "I learned about the high and low. I learned that prostitutes were doing it for the money and not because they were immoral, that they had kids or parents to support and could be likable. I was disappointed in many people I was supposed to respect and impressed with quite a few people I was supposed to look down on. Every day was a different day in the City Room. It was great for going to parties because I always had lots of stories to tell."

8

SPECIAL AGENT

ANY SANE PERSON MIGHT WONDER WHY Jack Grayson joined the FBI at all. It certainly was unlike anything he'd done before that late spring of 1950, and it arguably had even less to do with all he accomplished later. Still, he spent over three years of his life training to become and serving as a special agent of America's legendary law enforcement agency, the Federal Bureau of Investigation.

Jack was a less-than-exemplary FBI agent. From the start, he conspired—with the help of a woman he dated—to avoid the very accounting cases he was most qualified to investigate, those built on corruption and other fiscal malfeasance for which his education as a CPA perfectly suited him. Indeed, it was a signature of the FBI in the age of J. Edgar Hoover that agents often had law degrees or other advanced, specialized information that they used catching criminals—sophisticated criminals who spent their lives breaking rather sophisticated laws. Jack didn't want an FBI career based on accounting crimes; he wanted a career based on what he considered real crimes. That is, as it turned out, certainly the kind he got. And in Minneapolis, only about two weeks after showing up for his first posting, the crime became even more real than he had hoped.

Founded in 1908 under President Theodore Roosevelt, the agency that became the FBI was intended to be a Progressive response to the varied, often shoddy and sometimes corrupt police work found

across America, from city to city, town to town and county to county. The FBI Academy welcomed its first class in 1939 and soon took its place as what a twentieth anniversary history declared "the greatest law enforcement training center in the world." Even earlier, there had been a need perceived, especially after the Federal Crime Bill of 1934 authorized FBI agents to carry firearms and make arrests. Agents-in-the-making had to go wherever they could to perfect their skills, particularly to the firing ranges springing up as world war approached at military bases like Camp Ritchie, Camp Sims, Fort Washington and Fort Meade in Maryland, as well as at Fort Belvoir and the Marine Corps Base Quantico in Virginia. As the conviction grew that the FBI needed its own permanent facility, the Marines invited the agency to locate at their Quantico barracks. Hoover, by this time in charge since 1924, jumped at the opportunity.

With federal appropriation money in hand, the FBI was able to start construction and welcome the first class almost simultaneously. The original structure provided dormitory space for sixty-four men, two classrooms, dining and kitchen facilities, a gymnasium and a small gun-cleaning room and vault. Pearl Harbor sparked fresh interest in the FBI, especially as it battled subversives within this country, forcing the Bureau to increase the occupancy to 128 and then 176. In 1950, as Jack was arriving to start his four months of training, another addition to the basement and first floor was constructed, giving the young agents more dining, kitchen, gun vault and shop space. Jack was also in the first FBI class to enjoy air conditioning.

First and foremost, Jack remembers the weapons training—something that after growing up hunting in the South and then fighting for his life in the South Pacific came to him easily enough. In fact, one day on the FBI skeet range, a clay broke up and came out of the launcher in three pieces. Jack picked off each piece—one, two, three—to the amazement of his instructor. "I want that man on my team," the man said. Six decades later, Jack insisted, "It wasn't any harder than shooting quail in Fort Necessity."

There was practice at the Quantico firing ranges day and night,

using pistols, rifles and even machine guns—the kind FBI agents invariably used in the movies that sprayed targets with rapid-fire bullets. The hardest part was keeping the gun level as you fired, since the force of percussion kept trying to lift it up. Some around the Academy still referred to the pistol range to the right of the rifle range as the "Mud Flats," an outdated nickname since the area's paving during the war. So many young men were applying to the FBI that the Academy was building an auxiliary range on Chopawamsic Creek about a half mile away. Still, for all these ranges, some of the most memorable firearms training Jack received took place in the surrounding woods.

Using the technology of the time, the FBI mined the spaces formed by trees with targets that popped up when least expected. Going out into the woods at night, the agents-in-training were expected to be on their toes at all times. This, as it turned out, was a lesson Jack would learn less than perfectly. As he walked along trail after trail, shadowy forms sprang upward from the brush, forcing him to decide both "friend or foe" and whether innocent hostages were involved. He had only seconds to decide whether to fire at the target, and the results were not secret for long. "You are now dead," a recorded voice would announce. Or perhaps, "You just killed a hostage." It took no leap of the imagination to understand how crucial such split-second decisions would be.

When they weren't sleeping in the dorms, eating in the cafeteria or practicing on the range, Jack and his fellow agents were nearly always in some type of physical training. They ran up and down the Quantico hills—one of the steepest was known as "Cardiac Hill" and did countless push-ups, sit-ups and jumping jacks. Additionally, a huge amount of physical training went into all known varieties of self-defense. How to disarm an assailant in front of you with a handgun, how to disarm an assailant behind you with a handgun, how to disarm an assailant with a knife—these were everyday skills for FBI recruits, the goal always to make defense techniques second-nature so they were there in the arsenal when needed.

FBI man

Japanese-style martial arts encountered during the war, generally lumped together at the time as "judo," were part of Jack's self-defense training. In one of the stories Jack and other recruits remembered later with a laugh, the instructor placed them in a position so vulnerable all they could do was reach up and grab their assailant by his genitals. "You'll be in big trouble," the instructor laughed, "if he pats you on the head."

Jack learned to conduct raids on houses: how to move in swiftly and without mercy, deciding each moment whether the form flashing in front of him was a hostage or someone trying to kill him. And he learned two of the key rules of FBI training in those days: Never shoot a suspect in the back as he or she was trying to run away—better to let the suspect escape than do that; and always tell the suspect of his rights to an attorney and to avoid self-incrimination before interrogating him. This bureau practice was a mandate from Hoover at the very top, over fifteen years before the Supreme Court's *Miranda v. Arizona* ruling made those rights the uniform law of the land.

After four months at Quantico, Jack was ordered to Washington—to FBI headquarters within the Department of Justice—for two more

FBI training: studying tire tread

months of training. This training was different, though, most often in a classroom setting where points of law and other issues were discussed. Jack rented an apartment with three fellow agents from the Academy near the old Shoreham Hotel in DC and showed up at headquarters for the first time. He was directed to an open room with about twenty desks. And there, when he found his desk, were the two things that brought him here in the first place. For the first time, Jack picked up his official FBI badge and gun.

Not all of the next two months were spent indoors, however. In keeping with the FBI's chosen mission to undermine the communist threat in America, considerable time was spent learning surveillance. It started as simply as being sent to follow another FBI employee when he or she left the Bureau—to follow and not get caught—then to report back all details of where the person went from work, who the person saw and ultimately where the person lived. The fact that such assignments occurred day and night, rain or shine, was a fore-taste of the real FBI work to come. Jack could only count his blessings his time in DC was summer, without any blizzards to brave in the name of surveillance.

Another lesson Jack remembered well was people coming into classrooms without warning, under the guise of delivering a message to the instructor. Once they'd left, the agents were asked for detailed descriptions—height, weight, hair color, eye color, clothing and note-worthy habits. Again, the importance of such skills was not wasted on anyone in that classroom. Jack in particular was fascinated with how different the descriptions of the same person in the same moment could be, establishing the subjectivity within each person's point of view. "We realized," he recalled, "how little people actually see."

At the conclusion of his two months, Jack lined up with all the other new agents outside a large and elegant office. Each agent in turn was invited to pass in front of the desk and shake the hand of Hoover himself. The handshake only lasted an instant, but for a new FBI agent, it was hard to forget. "The joke was 'I'll never wash that hand again,'" Jack remembers.

Not surprisingly, during the DC stint much interest had gathered around where each agent would be assigned. Possibilities were part of many a late-night bull session fueled by no small amount of bourbon at the apartment. On the day they received their assignments, Jack and his three roommates took the envelopes home unopened. Each man opened his orders as though it were a present on Christmas morning. One roommate got San Diego and couldn't stop babbling about Pacific beaches and the señoritas in nearby Tijuana, Mexico. Jack and a fellow agent named Richard Ahearn were both assigned Minneapolis, far less balmy. It was understood that the Bureau be-lieved in sending agents to places they weren't familiar with, where their experience of something new and different would keep them alert and more able to pick out something amiss. As a Southern boy through and through, Jack in Minneapolis certainly appeared to fit the model.

Jack and Richard drove from Washington to the Twin Cities to-gether, finding an apartment on the Minneapolis side of the river across from St. Paul. Everything, in fact, seemed routine as they went into the regional headquarters, met their new Special Agent in Charge

(SAC in Bureau parlance) and settled into their desks to read the bulletins put in front of them. This they did without incident, or much interest, for their first two weeks in Minneapolis.

Off duty in their own minds (even though FBI agents were legendarily never off duty), Jack and Richard were driving in Richard's car one late afternoon, their guns safely stowed back at the office. They were searching for a liquor store along Lake of the Isles Boulevard, which Jack describes as a luxurious neighborhood, when a police car pulled up behind them with the siren screaming and the roof lights spinning. The men stopped, thinking they must have committed some small traffic violation. The police car raced in front of them and two men in plainclothes stepped out. Detectives, Jack thought in the moment, not uniformed patrolmen. Before he or Richard could enjoy one more thought, one man stood at each of their open windows, pressing a pistol to their heads.

"Move over or you're dead," the man at Richard's window said.

Richard followed orders, pressing into the middle of the front seat as the man climbed in behind the steering wheel. The other man got in the backseat behind Jack and pressed his gun against his neck. The man behind the wheel re-started the car and drove on. The agents saw that the driver was bleeding from the hand that held the gun on Richard, and the hand was shaking. It wouldn't take much for the gun to go off. They drove toward the outskirts of Minneapolis for close to an hour, much of it spent with the two assailants debating whether to "waste" their captives. It became clear to the agents that the men had earlier fired on police officers in order to steal their patrol car, and they feared one or more officers might be dead. They might not be, the man behind Jack argued, so that only by killing these two hostages now would the pair be facing Murder One. "Waste these guys," the driver said over and over, and Jack remembers wondering in silence, "Is this the way my life is going to end?"

Relatively good sense prevailed. The driver, frustrated at failing to convince his partner, pulled over to the side of the road and snarled, "Now get the hell out." In what has remained a logic defying

memory ever since for Jack, he responded, "I have some cleaning in the back seat. Can I get that?" "Yeah," the man said. "Quick." At no point had Jack or Richard mentioned to their captors what they did for a living, afraid that doing so would be a death sentence.

What they had to do was clear, even though they knew it would carry a price. Both understood Hoover's rule: Never embarrass the FBI. Jack and Richard had the distinct impression (accurate, it turned out) that headlines would follow, along the lines of "FBI Agents Kidnapped," with the subhead explaining helpfully "They Left Their Guns at the Office." The two flipped a coin to determine who would call the SAC. Jack won the toss, so it was Richard's call to make. They were ordered to appear ASAP, and every other agent assigned to Minneapolis was ordered in to hear what they had to say. Grabbing a ride from a driver who finally had sympathy, they made it back to the FBI office and endured the first of several grillings by the boss. At one point, in his office with the door slammed shut, the SAC put Jack and Richard on two extensions connected to J. Edgar Hoover and the attorney general. Hoover was noncommittal—his usual "just the facts" approach—and then thanked the two for the information.

Jack and Richard were sent home with orders to appear at the office the following morning. Obviously, their fates were going to be decided that evening.

They did learn, in all this talk, what had happened. Two former prison inmates, Winfred Meyers and Frank Edwards, had shot and wounded patrolman George Terp before stealing his vehicle and leading police on what the front page of the Sunday, September 17, 1950, *Minneapolis Tribune* called a "wild chase." The story mentions the theft of the car "privately owned by Richard H. Ahearn, FBI agent." Presumably Jack was fine with his own name not appearing until the jump on page fourteen. The story made a point of describing the agents as being "off duty" and "both unarmed." The two suspects were captured later, after what the paper described as "one of the biggest manhunts in the city's history." Jack and Richard were sent to the police station to confirm that Meyers and Edwards were their

captors. When that bit of business was done, the police asked the suspects if they had any idea they had kidnapped agents with the FBI.

"Oh shit," one of the men groaned, dropping his face into his hands.

Meeting with their SAC the following morning, Jack and Richard received new orders with the FBI's trademark deadpan delivery. Richard would take over the FBI's office covering the southern half of South Dakota from Pierre. Jack would take over the northern half, living out of a hotel and working from an office in Huron. "It was known," Jack says, "that the place you went when you embarrassed the FBI was Butte, Montana. It was well-known as the purgatory. This had to be better than that, I figured."

This time, the seasons did not work in Jack's favor. It was winter when he drove to South Dakota—a young agent still reporting to the SAC in Minneapolis, sent here as punishment, or at least a form of penance. The days were as cold and desolate as the landscape, and the nights were even more so. Jack knew not a soul when he arrived in South Dakota, and in the sense of lifelong friendship still knew no one when he left.

For all his sense of disgrace, Jack did find things to admire and enjoy during what proved his eight-month South Dakota exile. He did get to meet and essentially court all the local law enforcement in his area—men of limited education and knowledge of the larger world, trying to do a meaningful job on almost no money. He learned about Indian reservations, which as federal land were part of his jurisdiction. Even the most mundane crimes on a reservation—domestic disputes, public drunkenness, stealing a cow—were by definition FBI matters, and Jack was called out to investigate them all. Distances were huge, but in time Jack learned a useful trick. If he drove to the top of the highest butte, he could use his car radio to call each of the local "cop shops" in turn and determine there was nothing going on that was worth his attention. That, he decided, sure beat driving hundreds of miles across his turf just to hear the news.

One kind of case demanded Jack's personal attention—visiting the

area's many houses of prostitutions. Again, as in the French Quarter of New Orleans, he was struck by how real, human, everyday and sympathetic the prostitutes were. Many had been left with children to support by ne'er-do-well husbands, while others had health issues that kept them from pursuing more desirable employment. As an FBI agent, Jack had no interest in arresting anyone for prostitution. It was considered a state offense, if anyone there had bothered with it at all. His interest was the Mann Act, a federal law set in place to forbid the crossing of state lines "for immoral purposes." At each house he visited, Jack chatted with the new girls—asking them lightly where they were from, when they got to South Dakota, how they made the trip—and who paid their way. Either they all had paid their own fare or they'd been warned about agents like Jack. There were no Mann Act violations to be investigated. "I was beginning to like South Dakota as the weather warmed up," Jack recalls.

When the FBI finally decided they had suffered enough, Jack and Richard were both ordered to report to the large, busy Bureau operation in New York City. The crimes they were destined to deal with in and around the Big Apple would make the cold and desolation of South Dakota seem like child's play.

9

FIVE BOROUGHS

BETWEEN THE DAY JACK WALKED INTO HIS new office in 1951 and the infamous Appalachin Meeting in upstate New York of 1957 (by which time he was long gone), the FBI and organized crime enjoyed a strange relationship. It was so strange that, in later years, some would speculate that the Mob held dirt on Hoover's suspected romantic relationship with his assistant director, Clyde Tolson, and blackmailed the headman into silence. Jack had heard the Tolson rumors as far back as Quantico. In any case, silence was the FBI rule on such criminal activities by whatever name—whether it was the Mafia from Sicily, the Camorra from Naples, the Sacra Corona Unita from Puglia or the 'Ndrangheta from Calabria. At one point, Hoover famously declared that there was no such thing as organized crime in America. At least one young agent in New York City knew better, from his close encounters of the recent past.

Jack and Richard packed up their cars and headed for New York City, presumably leaving South Dakota undefended from communist threat for a time. With the familiar high rents of Manhattan, they found an apartment together on East 72nd Street, one smaller than anything Jack had lived in that wasn't a room in a hotel or motel. The bedroom was small, the bathroom was small and the kitchen was even smaller than that. It was also Jack's entrée into an exotic world he'd never really known. "The apartment was between the

slums and the rich people," he recalls. "And the people across the hall were Orthodox Jews."

Initially, Jack's assignment in New York involved catching the subway to and from the FBI offices in lower Manhattan each day and spending his shift reading and following up on pending cases and other communications until he was ready to head out into the streets and find his own. Worst of all, his life at the FBI was one big sign-in sheet. Sign in, sign out, over and over as the hours passed, and then separately logging everywhere he went, everything he saw and everybody he talked with. Having briefly experienced FBI life in Minneapolis, and then been on his own those eight months of purgatory in South Dakota, Jack found that his new life combined everything he'd disliked about the military with none of the rewards. Aboard the *Pasadena,* he had been truly defending his country, or at least staying alive another day. When he took time to think about it, Jack wondered if the FBI was the right place for him to be.

Upon arrival, Jack was given an area to cover: the Lower East Side and the often-violent South Bronx, which had come to be known in law enforcement circles as Fort Apache. Whenever he did hit the streets in those early months, it was generally to go there. Still, the suspects he spotted on his turf traveled throughout the day and night to all other sections of New York and across the river into New Jersey, usually with Jack using his surveillance skills not far behind. Before long, he was beginning to think that all five New York boroughs were his to cover.

In keeping with the times, the most serious crime he was assigned to investigate was communism, whether it took the form of measurable activity or merely sympathizing with the Soviet cause. From the perspective of J. Edgar Hoover on down, such crimes lurked in the very bloodstream of all society's malcontents, whether they were poor and Jewish on the Lower East Side or poor and black in the South Bronx. The latter group had cultural ties to a Harlem long past its Renaissance in the 1920s and 1930s, so Jack often found himself traveling far north of 100th street, usually keeping a close eye

FBI, New York

on someone riding the subway. On one occasion, alleged communists were gathering in central Harlem for a meeting thought to be significant; this time Jack took an additional agent and a car. Parked and waiting on the street to observe whatever happened next, the agents found themselves surrounded by small children chanting some sort of slogan.

It dawned on them, if slowly, that they were noteworthy enough as the only white guys on that street—and their suits, ties and hats only made the nature of their visit more obvious. The kids were chanting "L-A-V-A," over and over, mimicking the TV Lava soap commercials that accompanied a popular show about the FBI. Jack realized their presence or purpose in Harlem that day was far from secret.

Other full days were spent in Fort Apache itself, going into tall, dull, graffiti-covered housing projects to interview FBI informants or follow up on leads. Jack remembers feeling queasy and on edge each time he entered one of these dingy high-rises, knowing he had flight after flight of rank stairs to climb amid the groans of drug addicts and

the omnipresent sour stench of cooked cabbage. So many of these people had no jobs and no money, nowhere to go and nothing to do. For the young man from Fort Necessity, where the sharecroppers worked from dawn to dusk and only then relaxed over fresh-cooked food with their families, Fort Apache was a view of the lower depths of human existence that shook him deeply. Jack possessed not a communist bone in his body, but he found himself wondering what could be done to help these people or at least what could be done to help the country deal with them. For neither the first nor the last time, he thought of words like "dead end" when he looked at the people he had to interrogate.

The feeling was much the same, if not more profound, each Monday morning. Jack would start his workweek with a visit to the Bronx River Prison. The prison was little more than a holding pen for anybody picked up on any charges, or often enough no charges at all, over the weekend. It was Jack's job to go through the police blotter, much as he'd done as a cub reporter working the police beat, looking for names that meant something to the FBI. Sometimes those arrested were informants more important to the Bureau on the streets than locked up in a cell, and Jack would arrange with the police to release them. Other times it took a personal interview to determine if the FBI would be interested, and this meant going face-to-face with people writhing and vomiting during heroin withdrawal or beating their heads against the cell bars until they drew blood. Knowing that most of his efforts were for nothing, and that most of these men would be released without any charges being filed, Jack could never get out of the Bronx River Prison fast enough.

One of the most interesting cases Jack worked during his time in New York was a spin on grand theft auto. Expensive cars were disappearing off Park Avenue and turning up, the FBI quickly determined, in Miami. This was happening with increasing frequency, and yet regular police efforts to beef up their patrols didn't seem to be helping. Finally, one of Jack's informants let on that he might know something about it. The cars were being hot-wired and stolen in New

York, driven to a Mob-controlled "chop shop" in Astoria so the serial number on the block could be removed and then driven by a crew of young men to south Florida. There, other Mafia elements were happy enough to take the cars and sell them on the black market. With such guidance about the operation, the FBI in Miami was able to pick up one of the young men, who was more than happy to cooperate in return for a reduced sentence. It would be left up to that young man to worry about Mob revenge when he was released from prison.

During the interrogation, the Miami agents discovered that the man's mother not only lived in New York City but worked at the esteemed restaurant 21. They asked Jack to interview her for any insights she could offer and, since it seemed easier to catch her at work than at whatever might pass for home, Jack waited for night before putting in a call to the restaurant's manager. Yes, he said, the lady was working that night. So yes, Jack said, I'll be right over. Facing the young man's mother in a stark room, it became clear she knew nothing about the auto theft ring. Like all mothers everywhere, she insisted her son was a good boy and that it all must be some kind of mistake. If not, he must have fallen in with some bad kids. The mother was brokenhearted, Jack saw, as she punctuated her sentences with bouts of weeping. Jack knew the odds of this particular son being a good boy.

On the way out of 21, the manager stopped Jack and asked if he was off duty. Yes, Jack replied. The manager fixed Jack a drink or two, fed him dinner on the house and then took him around to meet celebrities in the dining room. Many Yankees baseball stars were there, along with a smattering of movie and Broadway stars mixed in with the wealthy clientele. Jack would ponder later what kind of strange day began smelling cabbage in the projects of Fort Apache and ended at 21.

The final movement in this auto-theft concerto took place in Astoria. It was time to shut down the chop shop and arrest whoever was caught there. After all, this was the closest the FBI would probably get to the Mafiosi behind the whole thing, since most of the kids

driving the cars to Miami knew little beyond the fact that they would be given a few bucks and a bus ticket back to New York. Jack knew well the Mob's tradition of *omertà*—telling law enforcement nothing, even when that meant going to prison—but he remained hopeful. In fact, no mobster would break the code of silence until Joe Valachi in 1963, but Jack and his agency superiors couldn't know that. That was how Jack ended up placing Dominick Alongi under arrest that day at the chop shop in Astoria.

Alongi was amiable about the whole thing, shrugged as though arrest was simply the price he paid for the business he was in—much as a New York cabbie had to pay for a license. He certainly put up no fight as he was led outside to a waiting car. In the months that followed, Jack's reports on the case helped send Alongi to federal prison. As feared, but also as expected, he never told anybody anything about the people who'd employed him.

Even as Jack began to wonder if his FBI career was meant to be long-term, his life in New York held many charms. For one thing, he was there at the heartbeat of so many things he loved—theater, opera, ballet. He made himself a regular at such performances, knowing they were not available everywhere. For another, he had embarked on a romance with a dazzling runway model who worked the high-fashion circuit in Manhattan but still lived with her parents in Queens. When the two weren't racing off together to a ski resort in southern Vermont, they were heading to Queens for Sunday dinner. And as so often in the past, it was the parents who started the slow drumbeat Jack hated to hear: "What are this boy's intentions? Don't you think it's time he married you?" The model clearly wanted to marry Jack, though she was able to insist it was her father's idea. And Jack didn't want to get married to anybody.

He had used many excuses over the years, and they evolved with his circumstances, from expecting to die in the South Pacific to having no job, no direction, no way to support a family. This time, as an FBI agent, all he could say was he wasn't ready yet.

At the FBI, Jack had again found himself entertaining literary

ambitions. He was hardly the first man or woman confronted by constant drama on the job to imagine it all written down. And he, after all, had something more than a modicum of talent. A magazine editor had told him so long ago, even while rejecting his short story. Jack started writing again, even as the FBI conspired to hand him a specific goal.

There was a magazine published for FBI agents, and in one more effort to boost their readership's loyalty and interest, the editors launched a short story contest. The top prize was hardly a windfall, perhaps $100, but the bragging rights of winning and being published in the magazine were huge. On top of that, wanting to win, Jack stumbled on an intriguing way to stack his personal deck. In time for the contest deadline, he wrote and submitted one short story under his own name, followed by another in the name of a fellow agent and two more under the names of agency secretaries. He did not think it necessary to inform them of their role. The results were rather impressive. The story Jack submitted as Jack took home an honorable mention, while the ones he submitted under other names came in first, second and third. Somewhere there lurks an official FBI photo of Jack's fellow agent Ed Utz—finally let in on his secret literary career—shaking the New York SAC's hand and accepting the first-place check for $100. Knowing that fair was fair, Jack let the three winners hang onto the prize money.

Counting the Academy in Quantico and the additional training in Washington, Jack had been an FBI agent for three years. He'd seen many of the mission's joys, including a feeling of camaraderie in the long, hard fight against perceived evils—a list led off by Soviet communism, as it would be for several more years. He'd battled crime both organized and otherwise, the very thing the FBI's director insisted did not exist in America, and come to appreciate both the drama and the sheer, numbing boredom of criminal life. And, being Jack, he had all he could take of signing in and signing out, of logging his every action and observation in case it should prove important in court months or years later. He knew, in his gut, that little he wrote

down in any FBI logbook would ever prove important to anyone anywhere.

He realized, in that way that happens in certain jobs, that he was through. There had to be something better to do with his particular, even his peculiar, set of natural talents and acquired skills. But try as he might in that small Manhattan apartment, he didn't have a clue how to figure out what it was. When it came time to resign from J. Edgar Hoover's Federal Bureau of Investigation, there was an entire world that might have something promising for Jack to do. But at that moment, there was only one place he could go.

Years later, walking along Royal Street in the French Quarter of New Orleans, Jack would suddenly hear a car screech to a halt behind him and the driver's door bang open. For one split second, he flashed back to all his FBI cases and wondered what bad guy had tracked him down to settle a very old score. Would this, Jack wondered as before, prove to be his final moment on earth?

"Hey," a gruff voice said. "You Grayson?"

Jack nodded, uncertainly.

"Well, Jack, I'm Dominick." Dominick Alongi was definitely smiling, putting out his hand for a shake. "I did my time, Jack. Now I'm living here. Making pizzas." Every Hollywood movie Jack had seen about such confrontations came crumbling down, and he found himself shaking Alongi's hand.

"And Jack, you gotta come have a pizza," the man said. "On me."

10

MEANING BUSINESS

THE DECADE-PLUS THAT FOLLOWED JACK'S resignation from the FBI—which he calls his "Muddy Period"—probably deserves a more positive designation. With so few verifiable milestones like college graduation or the Japanese surrender, his business and personal endeavors tend to run together in retrospect. Yet this also merely reflects that several of them, whether vocation or avocation, took place at the same time. The fact is that Jack entered his Muddy Period in a malaise, with no solid idea what he wanted to do or where he wanted to do it. As long as it didn't involve writing daily reports to J. Edgar Hoover, he was probably in. By the end of this period, however, he had solidified his career into one blending academics and business and had begun earning a national, even an international, reputation for doing so. He had become, in other words, Jack Grayson. But even at his "muddiest," he wasn't unhappy.

The farm in Louisiana, at first, was the only thing that mattered—unintentionally echoing Scarlett O'Hara, whom he had danced with at the premiere of *Gone with the Wind*. Still, it wasn't sentiment that brought Jack home to Fort Necessity but something more closely resembling an experiment. These 3000 acres filled with sharecropping families and still managed at a profit by Jack's father suddenly looked to him like a case study for Harvard Business School. With his father's blessing, the farm had dodged modernity at every turn when

possible, its only surrenders being the occasional mule replaced by a tractor. Jack was about to usher in the modern age of technology and management. He would learn some important lessons while he was at it.

Jack was able to convince his father and mother that Europe was calling. Several years had passed since their last visit, after all, and with an assist from the Marshall Plan, Europe had rebuilt from the years of war. The countryside, Jack urged his parents, would be lovely this time of year. Life was hard enough at the farm otherwise, and certainly profitable enough for the landowner, that such an extravagance was easy to justify. Jack's parents headed down to New Orleans to catch the first of several flights, and he settled into his parents' house. Then again, despite the big shoes he had set out to fill, to the sharecroppers he had known from infancy, he was still just "Mistuh Charlie"—the younger version.

Jack knew what he wanted to do. He wanted to introduce computers and management skills into running the farm, along with other management techniques he had learned about in graduate school. Yet even before he got serious about doing that, he got serious about continuing his own education—on his own, thanks to a comprehensive reading program from the University of Chicago called "The Great Books."

Night after night for nearly a year Jack settled in to read the Great Books. Compiled to be a chronological and thematic survey of thoughts that had changed the world—from today's understanding, "The Western World"—the program started with Plato and Aristotle and moved through thinkers like Thomas Aquinas to the great literature of the nineteenth and even twentieth century. Each night after his work on the farm was finished, Jack fixed himself a bacon, lettuce and tomato sandwich and settled in to read until midnight. He felt he had omitted the classics. And of all the books he devoured, he remembers one in which (to Jack's way of thinking) a mysterious man visits a prisoner in his cell and embarks on a discussion of whether that prisoner actually *wants* freedom. The prisoner becomes confused

and in the end remains behind his bars. Jack never stopped pondering this parable from Dostoevsky's novel *The Brothers Karamazov.*

"That has always been a struggle for me," Jack recalls. "All my life people had been telling me what I ought to be—you ought to go to church on Sunday, you ought to be in the military, you ought to have a good job. In other words, you ought to follow the rules. Most people don't really want freedom. They want authority and ritual, and they'll be very unhappy if you give them freedom. I don't believe that. I believe in freedom."

At the farm in Fort Necessity, each morning when he rose to manage its 3000 acres, Jack was enjoying—indeed, claiming for himself—precisely such freedom. He hadn't mentioned to his parents that, while they were making their latest Grand Tour of the Continent, he would be busy changing everything.

For one thing, what Jack saw all around him was inefficiency and a near-complete lack of accountability. Any good academic like himself, seeking to determine if the farm was well run, would have quickly smashed up against a lack of data. People worked, machinery was used, tools were taken out of the shed and, only perhaps, put back. Sometimes the borrower passed this or that tool on to a second or even third borrower. Sometimes a certain tool came to live at a sharecropper's house, not because it was stolen but because everyone knew that's where you went to get it. And naturally, any notion of measurable productivity, whether for land, for a tool or for a person, flew right out the window. How, Jack wondered, had his father ever been able to run a business so successfully in a manner that was so un-businesslike.

Within a few days, Jack started giving every machine and every tool a number, thus making it unique. The tractor formerly known as "Ol' Peg" or "the one with the busted whatever" became Tractor 12 or 16, with the numbers painted in a visible place. Thus it became unique and, in Jack's mind, trackable. Each tool was checked out like a book at the library and expected to be returned. The plots of land worked by sharecropping families also took on numbers, official from

ownership, not verbal or colloquial or voluntary. Until now, most plots were known by the people who worked it—sometimes, in the Southern way, named after people long gone from the land or even gone to their final reward. As Jack saw it, calling a plot the "John Purvis Cut" or "Preacher Hall's Cut" wasn't good enough anymore. How could anyone who knew anything about real business manage something like that? He identified every "cut" with a number.

There were other parts to Jack Grayson's Fort Necessity version of The Great Leap Forward. To view life as a professorial time-motion study, a person needs to know the time—and virtually none of the sharecroppers owned or ever wore watches. Jack bought watches for everyone and insisted they keep track of all farm activities by time started and time completed. And lastly, the workers had to be in communication with management and occasionally each other. Using a skill set he barely knew he possessed yet, Jack convinced Motorola to donate twenty walkie-talkies and build a tower to keep everyone in touch.

Being a researcher at heart—and a news reporter and an FBI investigator—Jack headed to the valleys of California and then the Midwest Farm Belt to see what others were doing. Some farms were modernizing along the lines he was moving at Fort Necessity; others seemed barely aware at all.

Jack's agribusiness revolution didn't work. By the time his father came back to the farm, every acre was littered with unintended consequences. Far from succeeding as "statistical analysis," the experiment fell victim to more variables than Jack had been willing or able to anticipate—most of them human. The workers couldn't or wouldn't do as they were told, finding a million excuses to revert to the old ways. The machines were impressive but even at the simplest level no one knew how to use them.

Relief must have been the feeling of the day when Jack's father returned to being master of the farm. All the improvements and modernizations were tossed aside, and the farm went back to the labors that had characterized it for generations. The project Jack had

grandiosely named CORTEL (for Computers Operation Research and Telecommunications) was a bust. Jack had learned never to discount the human variables underlying each otherwise logical vision. Unwilling to be Mistuh Charlie anymore, Jack headed to New Orleans to teach business at Tulane.

Beginning in 1953, Jack returned to the Uptown New Orleans campus of Tulane for a series of assignments that would fill most of the decade that followed, with time off for a series of entrepreneurial adventures and personal quests. The fact that he'd tried and failed to implement such things on the farm didn't, to him, bring their fundamental validity into question. If anything, he was more committed to both using these tools and encouraging their use throughout the next generation of America's business leaders. As an assistant professor at Tulane's School of Business Administration from 1953 to 1955 and as associate dean from 1961 to 1963, he felt he was doing precisely that.

The first of these forays was into an import-export business based in the World Trade Center overlooking the Mississippi River. The company was called O'Neill & Associates, and apparently Jack was the "associates." Looking back, he says he was drawn to the opportunity because it was "international," and he had always been fascinated with the ideas of doing business in other countries. He heard about the business, had a couple of meetings with the owner and signed on. "It was a two-man band," says Jack. "It sounded good."

In many ways, it was good. Nearly all the company's business was conducted by phone, Jack realized, so that allowed O'Neill & Associates to pretend to be larger and more substantial than it was. Sometimes this sleight of hand was natural and friendly; other times, to Jack, it plummeted into deception. The main work of the enterprise was selling huge cartons of canned goods—peas, green beans, carrots—to buyers in South America. Yet there was little the company could or would refuse to do. If a Latin client wanted to purchase enough of something, then of course O'Neill & Associates carried it. Maybe it was out of stock that week, but a shipment was due

in—having the Port of New Orleans start a few feet from the base of your building never hurt the illusion. There were other aspects to import-export that bothered Jack, however, especially the number of bribes he was involved in paying in order to do business in Latin America. When the president of Venezuela demanded a pony for his daughter just to negotiate, Jack found the man a pony, arranged for its shipment to Venezuela—and then started plotting a way out of this business.

The president of Tulane called Jack one day and talked about fundraising. Already, in the mid-1950s, universities had bought into the notion of donors as a way of stabilizing and expanding their revenues on top of tuitions, endowments and grants. Tulane, after all, was a private institution and could use a persuasive fellow like Jack Grayson to get donations from parents of students, alumni and local corporations. As he figured he wouldn't have to give anybody a pony, Jack took the job.

As assistant to the university's vice president for development, Jack was, as so often in his past, a New Orleans man about town. The same relationships he'd started building with Nigel back when he was a Tulane undergrad and later a newspaper reporter served him well. Again he spent his life amid the country clubs and Mardi Gras balls of New Orleans society, except this time he had a mission. This time he always had a business card, always had a brochure about the exemplary work Tulane was doing and always had a cocktail event coming up that those who were interested could attend. Building interest and excitement, playing off egos and uncertainties and never leaving without the check became Jack's daily bread. Some of these skills would remain important for the rest of his working life.

Considering the life he was living and the circle he was living it in, Jack's extracurricular passions tended to be large. He decided, for instance, to become a pilot and went out to New Orleans' Lakefront Airport (originally named Shushan, until the man of that name went to prison in the Louisiana Scandals) to find instruction. Jack became enamored with piloting small planes, since it met his personal

Cessna 175

requirement of being something new and involving a manageable element of risk. He would enjoy flying for years, eventually forming a partnership to buy a Cessna and keep it ready for weekend getaways. The only time he ever feared for his life in the air was flying up to Fort Necessity and getting caught between two violent thunderstorms, moving into one with another pressing from behind. Visibility was awful, and the effect on the physics that kept planes in the air was terrifying. Jack bobbed from 500 feet above Louisiana farmland with little idea where he was until an idea occurred to him clearly. He was heading north and the Mississippi River would be to his west. He located the river and followed it until the storm dissipated.

Horse racing became another fascination during Jack's years at Tulane—not surprisingly because it promised a role for his beloved statistical analysis. This time, Jack found himself studying the *Daily Racing Form*. Keeping his computer handy, Jack input everything he learned about a race at the historic Fair Grounds racetrack—each horse's bloodline, recent performance, the jockey and his recent performance, the all-important weather and track conditions—and out would pop the horse to bet on. Just as back at the farm, things were not always what they seemed. There was no way for a computer to forecast which horse would wake up with a leg cramp, or indeed which jockey would take a bribe to lose. In Jack's words: "You could never capture all the variables."

None of this understanding kept him from buying and racing his own horse, getting together with four other guys at a thousand dollars each and heading up to thoroughbred country in Kentucky. As

Portrait of Jack while at Tulane

they should have known, most good horses were going for $50,000 to $70,000 (though not today's millions), and they sat on their hands throughout the auction. Afterward, somebody told them about a yearling who had not made the cut for the auction but appeared promising. Since the advice came from a reporter who covered the Kentucky horse trade, it seemed worth a trip to see this horse. They bought the animal for their $5000, named him Nirboy and trailered him back to the Fair Grounds in New Orleans. Nirboy actually won his first race, clearly the highlight of Jack's career in thoroughbred racing. Before his interest would fade away against the backdrop of bigger projects, he would even try his hand at breeding racehorses at Fort Necessity.

Not surprisingly, as a Tulane development officer, a pilot and a racehorse owner, Jack met a lot of women. And he had long ago left his shyness with them behind him. It is not quite accurate, referring to matrimony, to say he was running out of excuses—some men, of course, never run out of excuses. What he was running out of was

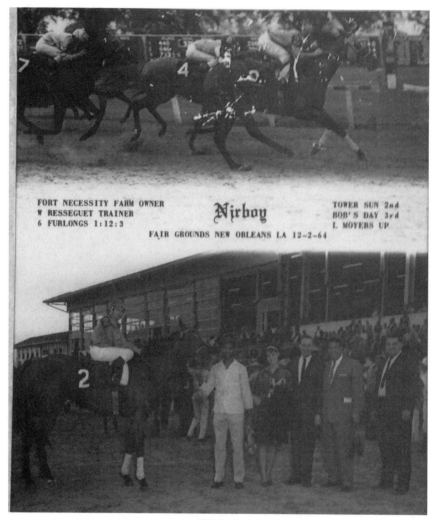

FORT NECESSITY FARM OWNER
W RESSEGUET TRAINER
6 FURLONGS 1:12:3

Nirboy

TOWER SUN 2nd
BOB'S DAY 3rd
L MOYERS UP

FAIR GROUNDS NEW ORLEANS LA 12-2-64

'Nirboy'

resolve. After all, he was pushing into his thirties, and not only were his parents and their friends all married but now most of his friends were married, too. You can only bring a date, he was learning, to so many events where other men are with their wives. It was only a matter of time before someone like Elizabeth Suzanne Burney walked into his life.

Betty, as everyone called her, was pretty, smart and sociable. The

two met, after all, at one of the numberless society functions Jack attended. They hit it off immediately, as people do when they're ready to get married and somebody promising shows up. With parents from Belgium, Betty was hardly part of the city's bloodline-focused crème de la crème, but she moved comfortably in such circles, as increasingly did Jack.

Their wedding in 1954 was a large and festive affair, with the ceremony in a church (though not the usual-for-New Orleans Catholic church, since Jack was brought up Methodist and Betty in the barely observant European Protestant tradition) and the reception in a hall nearby. Jack felt hopeful about all things that day: about being a married man and perhaps having children, about living in a lovely apartment not far from the Tulane campus, about continuing to pursue his vocations and avocations. Marriage felt like the right thing to do, just as married felt like the right thing to be. "They didn't have to drag me down the aisle," Jack recalls.

The couple was happy enough as newlyweds, though early on, as the joy of discovery started to wear off, they weren't as compatible as they had believed. They had a child who was diagnosed with Down syndrome shortly after delivery. Jack and Betty made the difficult decision to send the baby to a facility that specialized in such care until death came within months.

HARVARD YARD

LTHOUGH THERE WERE MANY THINGS Jack hated about academic life, his years of wearing different hats at Tulane showed him it might play a significant role in his future. He had earned his bachelor's at Tulane and his master's at the Wharton School of Business in Philadelphia. If he had any hope of building upward from those degrees, there was only one piece of paper left and one place to get it: a doctorate from the Harvard Business School.

It was beginning to seem Jack could have a job at Tulane as long as he wanted one, but as a man who would later make his first great research study and subsequent first great book about the importance of risk, this security was not what he desired. For Jack, it never takes long for safe to start feeling too safe. And besides, if he could stay at Tulane forever, teaching courses as he saw fit and working in other capacities as well, his value to Tulane would probably only rise with the addition of a Harvard degree to his curriculum vitae. Jack talked it over with Betty, and she seemed open to a move to Cambridge, at least for the year or two earning a doctorate might take. The program Jack applied for was relatively new and hadn't particularly caught on yet, so Jack was accepted on his first try. Harvard also liked that he was offering to serve as a paid grader for case studies written by undergraduate business students to defray part of his tuition. This made it possible for him to uproot Betty, load their belongings into a

U-Haul and head north without having to ask his father for financial support.

Initially, Jack and Betty lived in an apartment in Cambridge near Harvard Yard—the history-laden center of campus life. He studied between weekly thirty-minute face-to-face meetings with students to critique their papers. His comments, Jack remembers, were not well received. Some students already held bachelor's degrees from other universities. And some were getting nothing but As in other courses at Harvard, only to get an F from Jack Grayson, the grader.

One of his professors impressed and fascinated Jack so completely that the subject of risk became his dissertation. The professor was Howard Raiffa, a world-renowned scholar and mathematician who had already applied quantitative analysis and game theory to Las Vegas gambling, as well as to negotiating with the Soviet Union. It was exactly the sort of theory behind Jack's ill-fated efforts to modernize the farm—the use of data and computers to measure productivity with an eye toward making improvements. And it had increasingly been the aspect of business that attracted Jack's attention teaching courses at Tulane. It was time for Jack to study with the master. He asked Raiffa to serve as his dissertation supervisor. Jack marked the transition from taking courses to doing his own research by spending three or four months reading in Harvard's Baker Library, meeting with Raiffa one afternoon a week to go over any questions.

Tiring a bit of the bustle and the rent around Harvard in Cambridge, Jack and Betty found a rental house in peaceful Reading, north of Boston. It was the first time Jack lived in a house rather than an apartment since leaving the farm more than a decade earlier. This increased domesticity served Betty well. For one thing, she was able to get a job teaching elementary school in Reading. For another, she was able to seek guidance from a renowned fertility clinic nearby. She desperately wanted to have a baby, a healthy one who could remain at home and perhaps serve as glue for the couple. After examination, she was told that scar tissue was blocking conception. This was removed by surgery, and within a short time Betty became pregnant. Their son

Christopher Jackson Grayson was born on May 7, 1959. Betty was a mother at last. And while his mind and time were often elsewhere, Jack was a father.

The dissertation Jack was writing, grounded in all he'd learned from Raiffa, would require him to push the boundaries of knowledge and typical scholarship in several new directions at once. There was Raiffa's utility theory—a research method for getting a business person to reveal his risk preference. And there were personal probabilities and statistical decision theories—ways of analyzing the data gathered to see what it says about degrees of risk. Jack settled on the riskiest business he could think of—oil and gas. He would spend the next nine months flying between Logan Airport in Boston and the centers of that industry: Houston for the major corporations and Tulsa for the colorful wildcatters whose gutsy efforts pushed the industry forward. Fascinated by risk, by people ever ready to roll the dice, Jack made a few trips to Houston and Oklahoma City, but he made twenty to twenty-five to Tulsa. Wildcatters became the heart of his dissertation research.

"They were always what interested me the most," Jack remembers. "I remember one guy telling me he'd drilled eighty dry holes and was still going for eighty-one. For wildcatters, life is risk. It was obviously a thrill to them to live on the edge of great success and great failure. It got where it was a thrill for me to talk with these guys."

There can be no question that two of Jack's earlier careers—as a newspaper reporter and as an FBI investigator—helped him out when it came to interviewing oilmen in search of information. But it was his reading at Harvard that pressed him onto fresh turf, working with one wildcatter to construct a fictitious deal that he could then take to oilman after oilman, presenting it as though he were seeking their funding, talking over their questions about proposed risk and reward and then scoring them on their basic willingness. It sounds anecdotal, but with the encouragement of Raiffa back at Harvard, Jack managed to make it statistical. He also found himself pondering who played what role in judging the next deal that came through the

door. Some oilmen wanted to hear the pitch themselves, therefore placing people open to risk in gatekeeper positions. Others were satisfied with risk-averse people taking the first look. Thus the head guy never saw most of the opportunities that tried to come through the door. This fascinated Jack, seeing the way it worked in real time and real life, with real money, and a real company.

Jack also found himself pondering why large companies with well-defined corporate structures, such as the ones he visited in Houston, were reluctant to take on much risk. They felt more comfortable passing on something that turned out good than ending up with something that turned out bad. This seemed a contradiction to conventional wisdom, which held that large companies with immense resources could afford a solid gamble now and again. They could, he decided, but they seldom did. Those risks were being taken by the wildcatters he met in Tulsa and elsewhere, the kind of free agents who often went into partnerships with the major players—to enjoy their greater resources but save them from the inconvenience of facing financial ruin. Jack's affinity to these wildcatters is clear in the dissertation he wrote.

The work was so original, so intriguing, that the dean of Harvard Business School called Jack in and told him he should turn his dissertation into a book. Further, he said Harvard would be proud to publish it and offered him a three-year appointment as assistant professor. It took Jack another six months in Cambridge to complete the work. *Decisions Under Uncertainty: Drilling Decisions by Oil and Gas Operators* appeared in 1960.

The book, dust-jacketed in the closest thing a bindery has to a plain brown wrapper, is a testament to the days before university presses discovered they could publish works that would sell in the trade market—a process that, by many accounts, took off when LSU Press brought out John Kennedy Toole's novel *A Confederacy of Dunces*. The process has resulted in what some celebrate as broadening appeal while others denigrate it as dumbing down. Considering the number of graphs in its pages, there seems little chance that *Decisions* would have been embraced as bedtime reading.

As Jack saw it, the topic was decision making by business executives with an emphasis on the uncertainty aspect. The book describes how certain leaders make investment decisions under difficult conditions, prescribes techniques for becoming more rational decision makers and suggests possibilities for teaching these techniques. Specifically it deals with the fundamental question that always comes to the fore in oil and gas: to drill or not to drill. Part 1 of *Decisions* is descriptive, telling the things Jack had learned from operators at various levels, weaving in the main factors in their decision: geological, economic and personal. Part 2 of the book is normative, applying new and rigorous analytical thought processes to assist those who have such decisions to make.

Within the book's 400 pages, Jack does an impressive job of making the descriptive sound serious and the normative sound lively. In keeping with his own quirky sense of humor, he turns in his conclusion to a legendary head football coach at Notre Dame. "I'm not offering you a formula for finding oil or gas, either by chance or skill," Jack writes. "But I can't help but agree with the sentiment expressed in a remark attributed to Frank Leahy, 'Luck seems to go with the side that has the heaviest tackles.'"

Jack agreed, on the strength of his dissertation and book, to address the American Petroleum Institute in Dallas. His entire speech there ended up being preempted by one Lyndon Baines Johnson, who barged into the room to a raucous welcome from the oilmen. "I never got to present," Jack reports simply. *Decisions Under Uncertainty* was unquestionably a feather in Jack's cap, as a professional and as a scholar. Yet by the time the book came out, he had traveled a long way from Harvard Yard and was starting his next phase at Tulane.

Jack's star was rising in the business school firmament. For one thing, he had never lost touch with his old friends back in New Orleans at Tulane, and their conversations tended more and more toward Jack serving as dean of that business school someday soon. He resigned his position from Harvard after a single year with the intention of returning to New Orleans and accepting the dean position.

However, Harvard came with an intriguing offer for Jack to spend a year as a professor at their new business school in Switzerland.

Jack convinced Tulane to appoint an interim dean so he could spend that year in Europe for Harvard. Having driven his family and household goods in a U-Haul back to New Orleans for storage, Jack, Betty and Chris headed for New York to catch the *Queen Mary* to Southampton and a train from there to Lausanne via London.

The Harvard International Institute for Management Development (IMEDE, but known as IMD since 1990) was built by Nestlé beginning in 1957. There was an earlier similar and smaller effort called IMI, founded in Geneva by Alcan. The association with Harvard helped this time, along with the fact that Lausanne was a center of Europe business and business thinking.

"It was a plush deal," Jack remembers. Not only was he allowed to bring his wife and son to Europe with him for a year, all expenses paid, but he was to extend the same kind of offer to Tulane associate Gene Byrne as research assistant, along with his wife and two children. The Institute put the Graysons up in a nice house, living on the second floor above a Swiss family. Though all classes were taught in English, Jack quickly signed up to begin French lessons—it didn't seem right for a respected visiting scholar to know nothing of the local language. This also helped him complete further training as a pilot flying into and out of Geneva, seeing just how different two cultures' approaches to the same discipline and even the same equipment could be. The long, slow glides he learned as part of landing in the States wouldn't work in Switzerland, where in addition to the familiar panoramas of mountains there were big jets taking off and landing on the airport's single runway. The descent, therefore, had to be more of a plummet than a glide, and Jack enjoyed polishing his skills.

Working with executives from all over the world as his students, Jack was also able to hone his long-forming ideas about the whys and wherefores of business education. While he would often think across several disciplines, he could recognize that business education was also intrinsically different. Especially unlike liberal arts and many

Lake Geneva and IMEDE: Jack and Hungarian math professor visiting from Tulane

social studies, which tended to keep their graduates in a bubble of like-minded souls, often for their entire careers, business taught its students what it could and sent them forth. Their own futures, and probably the futures of entire corporations, would rest on what they knew and how they applied it.

Because of the Harvard Business School connection, all classes at IMEDE were taught using the case method. He came to admire its effectiveness, as his students researched real business moving through real situations and drew conclusions. What had Business X done right, what had Business Y done wrong, how could the situation have been handled better and what should be done going forward. Almost humorously, one of the case studies Jack chose to pursue involved the iconic Swiss watch-making industry, long treated on the world market as facing no competition. Watches were simply

who the Swiss were. In his class, however, this was an industry being strangled by too much tradition, about to be challenged by an upstart called Timex.

Within a few years, Timex was making watches in the United States that were cheaper, simpler and, for a time, more popular. The Swiss industry was forced to rethink what it did in order to survive, primarily as a super-premium product. The European students discussing the ins and outs in class couldn't believe such a thing could ever happen, but Jack saw it just over the next horizon.

The year at IMEDE was also important culturally and socially. Though Jack had met his share of Europeans in his various endeavors, he had never found himself surrounded by them. Dealing each day with students from France, Germany, Sweden, Italy and several other European nations, Jack was struck by how different they were from one another. It was hard for him to believe they shared the same continental identity—European—when their individual cultures made them even more incompatible than their utterly unique histories, ethnicities, languages and, in those days, currencies.

Additionally, there was the Organization for Economic Cooperation and Development (OECD), headquartered in Paris, still fresh from its success running the US-financed Marshall Plan that gave postwar Europe an economy to begin with. The OECD contacted Jack and asked him to conduct a study while he was on the Continent, assessing the needs of European governments and corporations and the ability of European business schools to use operation research. In conjunction with his work at IMEDE, this mission would establish Jack as one of the chief American experts on international business, a designation that would move his career briskly along for years to come.

In order to conduct his study, and making the most of his fresh understanding on the cultural divides, Jack paid visits to seven nations. In each, armed with the OECD mission and his Harvard Business School doctorate, he was able to get into all the major corporations and interview their presidents and CEOs. He was particularly

interested, of course, in their use of statistical analysis and operations research, such use as there was. On one memorable occasion, Jack and his assistant Gene traveled to Zurich to meet with the chairman of the International Bank of Switzerland. At some point in the conversation, both Americans noticed that the man was sitting up but fast asleep. They weren't sure what international business diplomacy would have them do, so they sat at the conference table in silence for what was probably ten minutes but felt much longer. Eventually the chairman woke up and continued as though nothing had happened.

Though much that was wonderful happened during the year Jack spent in Europe with IMEDE and OECD, it did mark the final break that led to his divorce from Betty. The couple continued to have arguments about many things, even in the alleged magic of their European idyll. As Jack describes it, Betty loved to go out on the town—and he usually did not, having grown tired of the evening social scene. Frustrated and unhappy, Jack struck up a friendship with pretty Barbara Schmit from Germany, who worked as a secretary at IMEDE. The friendship became an affair, and eventually Jack told Betty that she should go back to the States because he had decided to file for divorce as soon as he returned. Betty left, taking Chris with her.

As agreed a year earlier, Jack completed his assignments in Europe and returned to New Orleans to assume the business deanship at Tulane. Filing for divorce, he got his own apartment near campus and started making plans to ask Barbara (called "Muschi" or Little Kitten by her family) to join him. Eventually the divorce from Betty became final, Barbara made the crossing, and they were married in a small service at a Lutheran church in New Orleans. Over the next few years, Barbara would give Jack two more sons, Michael in 1968 and Randy in 1970.

With his Harvard and European credentials, Jack was able to take over the business school in New Orleans with a high level of support. There was the general feeling that he knew what he was doing and what he was talking about—especially when it came to international business, and New Orleans embraced anyone who made

$$E = hm\,c^2$$

Tulane

it feel like the center of a very large universe. Always averse to any person, place or thing that suggested it was an unimportant "backwater," New Orleans loved that its business dean was looked up to by leaders in more than a dozen countries. They were willing to give Jack's new ideas a chance.

Jack brought his global perspective and new ideas to the school as well as doses of New Orleans fun, like the time he brought two Playboy Bunnies to visit his accounting class. Jack desperately tried to think of how to tie the visit to accounting; in the end, he just drew a

modified version of Einstein's formula on the chalkboard. As Jack recalls, "The visit did nothing to contribute to the world, except having fun. Sometimes you have to break the monotony and have fun."

In general, Jack insists, the business school at Tulane didn't have any goals, other than continuing to be the business school at Tulane. That meant that his goals had some freedom to move forward, even if it also meant they would move forward alone. Not yet the education iconoclast he would become, Jack experimented with new kinds of courses, especially the statistical ones nearest to his heart, and new ways to look at professors. He learned, as though he hadn't known already, that he was up against many sacred cows in academia, including the tenure that kept professors in their jobs for decades and the research that kept their paychecks coming even when they were teaching few actual students.

Tulane was open to Jack's ideas, as long as they didn't shake things up too much. He had many arguments with his faculty members. Some resigned citing wrongs they felt he had done to them. Jack could have wished for nothing less, since moving forward got easier each time a roadblock was removed or opted to remove himself. Tulane looked on in bemusement as its dean declared open season for change. As Jack puts it without boasting: "Now I had power to do some things."

Early in his four years as the business school's dean, Jack made an acquaintance that would propel him to arguably the most visible appointment of his career. The Ford Foundation came to Tulane, asking the university to send someone to a commission it was forming to study what the nation's business schools should do to better address the future of international business in their curriculums. Tulane sent Jack to a series of meetings in various cities for long and rambling discussions with many other academics aimed at making recommendations in a final report. One of the commission members, George Shultz from the University of Chicago, found a kindred spirit in Jack. Before they knew it, much of their conversation was filled with their dislike of the slowness of academic life. All they did was talk, the two

business deans agreed, even when someone was expected to actually produce something. In a moment combining a whim and a wager, Jack and George agreed that, instead of a lifetime of meetings, the two of them should write the report over a weekend. This they did in New York City, meeting in the old Roosevelt Hotel. The report they submitted—and that won the commission's signoff—recommended that American business schools pay more attention to international business, create more courses so students could learn about business in other nations and ultimately study what other countries were doing in their own business schools.

A short time after the commission (a.k.a. Grayson and Shultz) completed their task, Jack was able to beat many of the same drums at a conference he organized under the Tulane banner in New Orleans. At his invitation, deans from about thirty of the best American business schools gathered to discuss the state of their international programs. George came from Chicago, continuing his warm acquaintance with Jack. It was a way to preach the gospel according to their report to the very audience who needed to become believers. It was also the last time Jack would see or seriously speak with George Shultz until he called on behalf of the Nixon administration to offer Jack a job.

Jack, meanwhile, wasn't merely teaching business. He talked the global accounting firm of Touche Ross & Co. into helping him create the Touche Ross Institute for Management (TRIM). With a naming sponsorship, TRIM sent faculty members from the Tulane and Stanford business schools to Europe each summer to teach them how to use the best business tools with executives based there. Courses were taught all over Europe, from Spain, Belgium and Germany to Denmark and Norway, and the faculty members received high marks from their students for the increased awareness they delivered.

By 1967 and 1968, Jack took trips to the Stanford Business School to teach international management to their business executives during summer programs. And while there to teach and learn about business management, he and Barbara wanted to know more about the nearby hippie revolution in the Haight-Ashbury district

in downtown San Francisco and also Esalen, the site on the Pacific Coast Highway where seminars were provided to experience the social revolution—sensitivity training, yoga, meditation. One of the senior Stanford business school faculty warned Jack about talking too much about his experiences to other Stanford professors—it was still considered too far out. Still, as a scholar, Jack recognized a real movement when he saw one, a real change, and even in New Orleans and eventually Dallas, he wasn't surprised that ripples from the Haight would later be seen. It's hard to say exactly what Jack gained for his academic or personal life from such sessions, but as he puts it impishly, "It was stimulating."

As the school year of 1968 neared its end, Jack took a phone call from Dallas in his office. The caller was Ed Cox, known to Jack as a wealthy Texas oilman, and he was calling on behalf of Bill Clements, who would later serve two terms as the first Republican governor of Texas since Reconstruction. Would it be all right, Cox asked, if he and Clements came over to New Orleans to meet about an interesting opportunity.

Once they were behind closed doors in Jack's office, Cox and Clements pulled no punches. The business school at SMU was in dire straits, they said, near the bottom of any list. Why, they asked, in a city known for its aggressive, high-risk, wealth-creating approaches to doing business every single day, would the best-known business school be an embarrassment? SMU was ready to make some big changes—any changes Jack wanted—with enough support, time and, yes, money, to make the changes stick. The salary the two men offered him was nearly double what he was making at Tulane, a place where even his smallest administrative changes were treated as frightening major surgery.

"Well," Barbara said when Jack told her about the offer, "why don't we try it?" So they did.

To help with the revolution that this effort would require, Jack asked his trusted colleague, Gene Byrne, to accompany him to SMU. Gene had worked with Jack at IMEDE and Tulane and shared Jack's views about student-centered learning.

No one could yet guess the width or depth of the changes Jack would call for as new business dean at SMU, with the possible exception of right-hand man Gene. Jack's first request was to change the color of the institution's dome from dull gray to gold, "because all the other domes at SMU were gold, and I didn't want the business school to look inferior." "They knew I'd make waves, do innovative things, and they wanted me to," Jack offers. "But really, they didn't know how revolutionary my ideas would be."

12

GONE TO TEXAS

BEGINNING IN 1968, THE NEARLY THREE years Jack Grayson spent as dean of the business school at SMU were an adventure, an experiment and a crucible. Despite the initial carte blanche of Bill Clements and Ed Cox when they recruited him, the years were, more than all three of those things put together a revolution and a war. Jack was a radical education visionary invited to carry out his ideas in perhaps the least radical, least visionary environment on the face of this earth: a well-established American university.

Before this period would come to a close with an unexpected invitation from the Nixon administration, Jack would excite some students and frighten others, terrify many administrators, threaten veteran faculty members and even incur the wrath of an academic association that gives colleges and universities their accreditation. If Jack had set out to shake academic life to its foundations—instead of, in his mind, simply making the system work better—he could not have done a better job. The debates he engendered, sometimes single-handedly, cut to the heart of what a university is, what it's supposed to do and who it's supposed to do it for. Some of the debates continue to this day. It is remarkable, in retrospect, how matter-of-fact Jack was about his intention to radically change an educational belief system that had been respected, obeyed and codified for hundreds of years.

As a reality check, however, it's worth noting that the three most

important sacred cows Jack tried to end—required curriculum, prerequisite courses and faculty tenure—remain secure parts of nearly all college campuses in America. The fact that Jack was a business expert heading up a business school didn't mean, to many faculty, that he should run that school as though it were a business, though Jack would say it's the only way for real learning. There were simply too many traditional forces at work in a traditional university, too many outmoded traditions, too much emphasis on teaching rather than learning and too little responsibility given to the students so they could learn how to learn. Since his actions were all based on ideas that seemed to fit within his mandate, it's worth considering each idea on its merits along with why Jack had come to hold it among his deepest convictions.

His first thought was how could he get the entrenched, powerful—and in some cases incompetent—faculty to change. He tried two ideas. One was the use of a popular technique called "The Managerial Grid" a successful methodology for plotting individuals on a two level grid. Vertical numbers indicated an almost total focus on people while horizontal numbers were an almost total focus on results. So, a 1-9 was an almost total focus on humans, and a 9-1 was almost a total on results. When asked to participate in this process, the traditional faculty refused. Jack then tried "sensitivity training" he learned at Esalen with faculty and students locked in a room for several days just talking with no agenda—just conversations about what was going on in the room. The faculty refused to participate. By this time, Jack gave up on persuading them to change by softer methods and started to use rougher methods.

Curriculum, understandably, lay at the base of his proposed changes. To Jack, if you wanted to turn out a different and more successful type of business school graduate, you absolutely had to change what you taught and how you taught it. Perhaps even more radically, in Jack's vision, you had to change the way all such decisions were made. Even now, the idea that students should decide what they learn and how they learn it seems decidedly heretical. What would keep

young people, after all, from always choosing the easiest road and emerging with an education that included little if any actual learning about business? Yet when Jack looked out at the men and women walking around the SMU campus, he saw precisely the people who should have the freedom to shape their own destinies: the students. Quickly, as dean, Jack took aim at the two primary ways universities tell students what they must study.

The first took the form of required courses, which in any discipline made up the bulk of the credit hours a student amassed in pursuit of a specific degree. The second took the form of prerequisites, meaning basic courses that had to be taken before a student could enroll in more advanced courses. Both, it seemed to Jack, robbed a student of freedom. And both, he decided, had to go.

To accomplish his goals in a business school setting, it was not enough that Jack was dean. There were procedures to be followed, and Jack set about following them—with his eyes ever focused on the prize. To do away with required courses, for instance, there had to be a vote of the Faculty Senate, an august and tradition-laden body on any campus. From the start, Jack used the extra funding pledged by Clements, Cox and others to lure similar-minded professors to SMU from other universities and businesses. Apart from having excellent teachers, this also meant he'd have votes likely to go his way in the Senate. He also, in a move that seems even more dramatic, invited promising students to sit and vote on the Faculty Senate. While it fit his vision perfectly, the notion that even the most rarified ivory tower would include some of the young people it sought to educate both horrified and enticed. It also delivered votes.

Like any master of the legislative process, Jack carried around *Robert's Rules of Order* and counted his supporters in the SMU Faculty Senate day after day. Encouragingly, even some of the current SMU professors came around to understand and find something of value in all he was saying. Gene Byrne was also of immeasurable help in securing the votes. When Jack finally knew he had the votes, he brought the change up for a decision and carried the day—by a

Dean, School of Business Administration, SMU: 1968

single vote. Required courses were no more a part of the SMU business school, nor were prerequisites. Faculty would advise students in their choices but not dictate them. Students would pursue the areas that interested them, if when, in theory, they had little to do with a particular or traditional business discipline such as accounting, marketing or human resources. It was Jack's belief that most students would choose the courses they needed and that these courses would be remarkably similar to those some traditional professors might force them to take. The difference would be that the students would choose and accept the responsibility for their learning. And that difference would mean everything.

Equally essential to Jack's way of running the business school was the abolition of tenure, and nothing would make him as many enemies as that. He wanted to offer professors five-year contracts, renewable on performance. He announced his intentions to do so but left SMU before he was able to carry them out. He might have stayed twenty years and never managed it, considering the forces that gathered against him.

The notion is simple. Tenure—the concept that once a professor

had earned it at a university, he or she could not be fired—had been created by those who believed it protected the integrity of the teaching itself. Like all things that protect or guarantee employment, it lifted an employee out of fearing change in his job—change of management, change of politics. Tenured professors were, much of the time, the most respected members of any faculty. Indeed, tenure was the thing young faculty members worked to achieve above all else, typically by conducting original research in their field and by publishing papers through the time-honored process of peer review. At some level, tenure worked well for the education process, and it still does. Jack, however, felt that the bad outweighed the good.

Some of the most distinguished faculty members barely interacted with students at all, leaving the mundane act of teaching to their graduate assistants; keeping only irregular office hours to advise students, answer their questions and address their concerns; and generally following a top-down model. This was the position they'd studied, written and worked for years to achieve.

In place of tenure, Jack proposed a contract with faculty similar to many in the business world. Clearly, this was an arrangement that allowed no resting on laurels and definitely no slacking off—with clear measurements of performance and fair ways of assessment. And in place of research, in place of academia's publish or perish philosophy, Jack's employment proposition emphasized teaching in the classroom and accessibility in the office. With students, rather than faculty or administrators, now organizing their own courses of study, professors had to be there when needed, not merely when convenient. There was a suspicious whiff of customer service about the arrangement as though professors actually served, actually provided a product to their students, rather than sat daily in their offices to be visited only when a supplicant figured out how.

So many controversies swirled, almost daily it seemed, around Jack's extreme policy disruptions that less attention was paid to his plans for the physical space. At an older school like SMU, the building was the building until you could raise money to build a new one.

Even within that existing structure, Jack's published ideas now seem as radical as anything he was advocating in regard to faculty-student relationships. In Jack's view of this business school, form would definitely follow function.

Anyone who's been on a traditional university campus can describe virtually all of them, and their design is purposeful. There's a building, usually a blockish one with steps out front, and then some stairs inside to however many floors there are. The bulk of the square footage is taken up by classrooms large and small, mini-Greek theaters with some sort of podium or desk where the stage might have been and rows of desks or chairs circling outward across the room. Other spaces contain small, usually book-cluttered faculty offices, which usually are empty and have their doors locked. And still others contain administrative personnel, the people in charge of all things who are protected in offices behind an open area filled with secretaries who take messages. In his head, Jack was drawing a quite different design, one that wouldn't be fully realized until he built a new building to house APQC some years later.

In a report prepared about SMU in 1970, as well as in several magazine articles, Jack let his innovation flow, perhaps most strikingly when it comes to the use of space. "Remove most of the interior walls inside the building offices and administrative spaces," he wrote. "Create closed spaces only as an exception for specialized time and things requiring privacy. Create individual workstations for every student. Enliven the learning spaces with color, information, displays, plants, audio-visuals." That last bit of the proposed décor connects with Jack's awareness of the still-newborn technology revolution. His dream business school would be wired to support computers, video and telephones, and it would also feature electronic links with other schools, businesses and all levels of government for sharing best practices. "Best practices" was a relatively new concept in the business world at that time, one that would still be in use four decades later.

All these changes, made and proposed, required one thing above

all others—and Jack came to call that thing "acculturation." In fact, he designed a course around it for students new to his school and set down his "scattered thoughts" on why. Defining acculturation as learning to accept and eventually embrace constant change, the course Jack created invited SMU business students to do nineteen things, among them "to learn to live in and to grow organic forms of organization," "to build a culture in the business school that is not antithetical to the culture in business" and finally "to learn to be entrepreneurial and achievement oriented." Acculturation ended up being the only required course at Dean Grayson's business school.

In pursuing his goals and his visions, conflict became Jack's daily bread. It became so as well for unintended victims of his "education revolution"—the university administrators—who often could only scratch their heads and try to limit the damage. Some of the business school's tenured professors wrote "poison pen" letters to the administration and even to the Dallas business community. If this dean has his way, they warned important employers like Neiman Marcus and SMU would cease to produce graduates ready for employment in their offices. And before long, such lone voices were joined in a chorus conducted by the American Association of University Professors (AAUP) and eventually the Association to Advance Collegiate Schools of Business (AACSB).

Both of those organizations existed to support, encourage and protect from harm the ongoing process of educating students. But to Jack, each in its own way came to represent the forces that resisted change. The first was the AAUP, which had the express purpose of helping its members hold onto their laurels, their salaries and indeed employment itself. The AACSB granted or denied accreditation to business schools, thus giving them an important tool in marketing and recruiting. The AAUP threatened to "blacklist" the SMU business school, making it impossible for Jack to hire its members. And the AACSB threatened what most felt was the darkest punishment of all—disaccreditation. As Jack admitted in one of his papers of that time, "I've succeeded in one way or another in antagonizing almost everybody."

In meetings with those two groups, as with the administration, as with faculty and students, Jack's message was always a variation on this theme. This makes sense, he told them. This will help business *and* education. Everyone will, in truth, be better off with more freedom. Or as he put it decades later, "I believe in a world where people choose freedom." Students, in general, came around to his view more quickly than professors, since the latter had more to lose. Eventually, through discussion, compromise and the simple process of showing his changes were working, Jack staved off both blacklist and disaccreditation, though it's unclear what would have happened had he stayed his course at SMU a few years longer.

Two major incidents in Jack's life capture the forces at work perfectly: one involving Dallas billionaire (and later third-party presidential candidate) H. Ross Perot and the other a brilliant professor Jack hired named Pat Canavan.

At one point in Jack's time as dean, Perot heard how he was shaking things up—like many businessmen, Perot considered this an improvement—and offered the school $50,000 to study what it ought to do next. Jack said yes to the grant and also to Perot's stipulation that it not be spent anywhere else in the university. The money was to be used to study which improvements to make with an eye toward a larger gift—which Jack suggested as $12 million—to actually make the improvements. Two other business schools, Perot warned, were getting the same opportunity to compete with the big check going to whichever one developed the best plan.

Jack spent all of Perot's $50,000 doing what he had always done best, traveling the world to meet with business leaders and bringing home their brightest ideas. Later this would be called best practices benchmarking. He went to Belgium to talk with Reg Revans about action learning, which suggested moving executives from one industry to another to teach them to learn in different settings. With selected faculty members (those not fighting his programs), Jack visited other business and engineering schools, assessing their ideas and innovations. Along the way, Jack set up the Institute of Entrepreneurship,

within which students could start businesses of their own—for class credit. He raised money from a Dallas businessman to bring in a professor from MIT to run the program.

When Ross Perot's six month challenge came to an end, Jack and his senior faculty made a presentation to Perot and his sister who managed his foundation. Jack believed that the Perots were positive about what they had presented, but no decision was made until they had seen the presentations of the other challenged schools. It was then—in this interim period—that Jack got an unexpected call from George Shultz, now with the Nixon administration. Jack quickly asked Perot if he could wait until Jack finished his new government post to make his final decision. Amazingly, and in testament to Jack's skills and merit, just as Tulane had agreed to postpone the deanship years earlier, Perot agreed. Ultimately, when Jack returned to SMU two years later, that funding fell through when SMU could not secure donors to match Perot's funding.

If the Perot story was about money, the Canavan story was about academic freedom, set against a time in which the feverish sixties zeitgeist that had already convulsed campuses up north was finally, slowly, making it to the South. By way of credentials, Pat Canavan had actually been at Woodstock. Additional credentials, according to Jack, included a record of innovative teaching at Yale and having "a ponytail down to his butt." Canavan even removed the door from his office, ate lunches at his desk so he wouldn't miss a student stopping by and suspended a parachute from the ceiling. "What color is yours?" he'd always ask visitors, referencing a business bestseller of the day. Canavan was perfect in this new world, and he joined Jack in such announcements as installing an inflated geodesic dome around the business school's entrance on Parents' Day and playing what was then called acid rock throughout the entire meet-and-greet. "We had," Jack remembers with a grin, "a semi-Woodstock adventure."

The only immediate downside was a phone call from the university chancellor, who asked that Jack not create such a popular attraction at future Parents' Days. "Nobody came to my tea party," the

SMU: Professor Pat Canavan in the geodesic dome: 1968

chancellor complained with good humor.

Parents' Day attracted attention to Jack and his hippie-looking protégé, which attracted, naturally enough, the SMU newspaper. In an interview, Canavan had the nerve to criticize how American businesses were often run, asserting that many of them were "pretty shitty." Perhaps it was a different time, or perhaps it was the conservative nature of a university founded by the Methodist church, but Clements and Cox visited Jack right after the article appeared, giving him a simple choice, either he would go or Canavan would. The decision was his to make within two or three days, and it was a painful one. A version of student protest arose around the academic freedom issue, with posters all over campus, marches and attempts to occupy the administration building, even PBS interviews. In conversations with Canavan, Jack offered to resign with him. The professor brushed this suggestion aside, said he'd resign because he'd been wanting to spend time in the north woods anyway, and even grabbed a bullhorn and talked the protesters outside into going back to their books.

For twenty years, Jack heard nothing of Canavan's dealings or whereabouts, though he certainly remembered the man and those

turbulent times. Finally, in a meeting with the chairman of Motorola on behalf of APQC many years later, the chairman invited one of his associates into the room and told Jack, "I think you two know each other." It was Pat Canavan, minus the ponytail. According to the bio on his much-later website for Canavan Consulting, the former professor held significant positions with Motorola in Europe, the Middle East, Africa and the United States from 1980 until 2008, focusing on leadership and organization development, globalization, corporate governance and mergers, acquisitions and dispositions. The bio mentions Yale and later the University of New Hampshire (with its Center for Industrial and Institutional Development), but says not a word about SMU. By all evidence, the north woods had agreed with Pat Canavan.

George Shultz, at various times secretary of four different Cabinet-level agencies (Labor, Office of Management and Budget, Treasury and State), was also an academic colleague who had worked with Jack when he was still at Tulane. Jack heard from him infrequently but thought nothing much of it when a call from Shultz came through to his office at SMU, out of the blue. All he could say was, "Good to hear from you, George."

"I'm calling on behalf of the President."

Jack still remembers stopping himself before blurting out, "President who?" or "President of what?"

"He wants you to come up here and run price controls."

For a moment, Jack struggled with what that might mean. The first question that came to mind, however, wasn't how but *why*.

"Now George, you know I don't believe in price controls."

"I don't either," Shultz replied. "But the President has decided he wants to create price controls. And he's letting me pick the person to run it. And that's you, because of your belief in the free enterprise system."

The rest of their conversation that day was brief, since Shultz knew almost as little about what should or would happen next as Jack did. The whole thing was free-form at this point, little more than

a notion really, that controlling the prices businesses could charge for their products would curtail the inflation that had been chewing away at American incomes and buying power in a way that was bad for the economy—and even worse for presidential politics. Jack asked if he could have about a month to settle his affairs at SMU.

"I can give you three days to get up here," Shultz said.

With his plans to relocate to Washington, Jack was suddenly facing the very types of change he had preached to students and faculty alike. He wasn't sure what he was getting himself into as the nation's first (and apparently last) peacetime chairman of price controls, but he gathered that the hours would be long and the work intense, surrounded by the likes of President Nixon, George Shultz, Donald Rumsfeld and Dick Cheney. In response, he rented his wife Barbara and their two small children a comfortable house in the artsy Mexican hill town of San Miguel de Allende, planning for Barbara to pursue her own art and Jack to visit as often as he could.

He knew he would return to SMU at the end of his time in Washington but, based on all that had gone before, wasn't sure under what circumstances. He appointed one of the faculty, Bobby Lyle, as his interim successor. Lyle would later make a fortune in oil and gas and end up serving on the APQC board of directors. With Jack's family settled in San Miguel and solid leadership in place at SMU, Jack was as ready as he could be for the new challenge. Yet he never forgot what he tried to accomplish at SMU, even with so many mixed results. In fact, these efforts would form and fuel most of what he would do in life from this moment forward.

"SMU was my dream of how people should learn and behave in education," he says. "And to this day, nobody does what I was talking about. Some of the reforms stuck, but most returned to their original form like a rubber band. The SMU business school is still accredited. There are required courses in place again. Tenure was diminished but never abolished. Still, I can take some pride that tenure now is not just for doing research but for being a good teacher."

While a rocky road at times for Jack, SMU also took pride in its

relationship with him, and in 2006, he was honored for his leadership and innovation with endowment gifts and naming stipulations from Bobby Lyle to the SMU Cox School of Business. SMU established an endowed scholarship in entrepreneurial studies for MBAs and also launched an annual innovation award for faculty in Jack's name.

13

THE PRICE OF CONTROL

J ACK GRAYSON'S FIFTEEN MONTHS AS THE
nation's only "price czar," or more formally as chairman of
President Nixon's Price Commission, ended up being "the
toughest, most challenging, most exciting and most interesting job"
he ever had. Oddly perhaps, Jack remembers being paid for his efforts,
but with no idea how much or how little he got. Even more oddly, it
all began with that unexpected phone call from George Shultz.

In retrospect, the whole fifteen-month adventure seems a bit hal-
lucinogenic, starting with the vision of a Republican president mov-
ing to control the free enterprise system normally so central to the
GOP. But it was more complicated, and perhaps more understand-
able, than that. Nixon had already imposed a price freeze across
the board in the nation. So the goal of Jack's newly formed Price
Commission was not so much to keep prices on almost everything
from going up as to find a logical, defensible way of letting them rise,
but only enough to control inflation at its then current level of five
percent, with a real goal of reducing the inflation rate to closer to two
percent. While the inflation rate was constantly fluctuating during
the period, Jack was nimble and succeeded in cutting the inflation
rate by half during his tenure.

As a passionate believer in free enterprise, Jack faced a choice
between turning down the appointment and trusting himself to be
the person who could do the best job for the country. He chose the

latter. Within days, he was getting advice from everybody he knew, and within weeks he'd be holding meetings to gather more. Little of it, however, rose above the words of George Shultz in that first phone conversation: "Why don't *you* think of something, Jack?"

Phase I was the price freeze, in the parlance of that time. Therefore, Jack was being called in to manage Phase II, during which systems and measurements would be put in place to decide when and if to let prices edge upward. Before the end of his fifteen months, Jack would be caught up in discussions and disagreements about Phase III. But by then his resignation was heading for Nixon's desk.

His family safe and happy in San Miguel, Jack flew into Dulles Airport to start his new job. He was met by a long, black car with several men wearing suits inside—a service that would be available to Jack 24/7 during his time as a government executive at the Cabinet level. The car took him to what was then the Shoreham Hotel, where he reached his room just in time to hear TV newscasts announcing he was the nation's new "price czar," a bit of journalistic shorthand that the Chairman of the Price Commission would have to get used to. He was told to be ready for pickup in the morning for a meeting at the White House. For the first time, seeing his headshot on the hotel TV, did he realize what a position of national visibility he had accepted.

The White House meeting at the very first part of the morning did not include Nixon, but it did put Jack in front of two of the President's advisers, Rumsfeld and Cheney. Donald Rumsfeld quickly made clear that he was Jack's prime contact within the Cabinet, the funnel through which information could be sent upward to the President or instructions sent back down. Yet also there was Rumsfeld's aide Dick Cheney. As usual, everything was positive at that first meeting, the presumption being that political ball would indeed be played. It was the Washington way, even though Jack admits understanding it little at the time.

The first time he saw Nixon in person was moments before the President called a press conference at the White House that same morning to announce Jack's appointment. When Jack walked into

the Press Room, it was filled to the brim with reporters and TV cameras. After alluding to some of Jack's credentials as a scholar and business dean, Nixon said something about "utmost confidence" and motioned Jack toward the microphone.

"Here I was at the White House with a room packed to capacity with reporters, all asking me questions. The first question was who I voted for in 1960, and I said Kennedy. They wrote that down. And then somebody asked me who I voted for in 1968, and I said Nixon. They wrote that down too. Then somebody else asked me if I was a registered Republican or a registered Democrat, and I said I was an independent. I saw somebody race out of the Press Room, and I figured he was going to check how I was registered. I always knew only one way to talk to the media, the straight truth as I understood it. And I could tell I'd better stick to that, as every word I said would be checked and rechecked. It helped, I'm sure, that I had been a reporter too."

Getting to Washington as quickly as he'd been ordered to, Jack arrived ahead of the office building at 20th and M Streets that would house the Price Commission and ahead of any staff. This Jack discovered when he asked where all his people were, only to be told there weren't any yet. He would have to find them, probably elsewhere within the government—detailees from most of the other agencies. Two early godsends were Louis Neeb, a senior civil servant who would later co-author the book with Jack titled *Confessions of a Price Controller* and Dick Feezle, a "real get-it-done guy" from the OMB—Office of Management and Budget. Dick's first question for Jack was whether he understood all the layers of rules governing government employment. When Jack said he didn't, Dick said, "If you don't mind violating all the rules, I'll get you several hundred people. Don't ask. They'll just show up."

Within days, the flood of people began—groups of ten or twenty at first. Within weeks, the flow grew wider and deeper, even as the construction and other crews plastered walls, put in carpet, installed telephones and addressed the thousand other items that appear on

Price Commission Economic Data Review (Jack, center of table in dark suit)

any bureaucrat's punch list. Jack lived a few days at the Shoreham, then moved into a room at the University Club at the beginning of Embassy Row and finally rented a one-bedroom apartment in the same area. After all, he knew he wasn't going to be home very much. As for meals, he remembers eating lots of canned corned beef—and putting on weight.

As more people showed up from somewhere else day after day, Jack had a suspicion he finally got around to asking Dick: "If you were a government agency," he asked, "and somebody asked you to send over X number of people, wouldn't you send, well, the less gifted and the troublemakers—the people, in other words, you wanted to get rid of?" Dick's answer was "Absolutely." And that notion fueled Jack's very first address to the staff of the country's first peacetime Price Commission.

"I don't know any of you," he said, members of the staff gathered all around him. "I have no assumptions about your past. I've been told the other agencies will pick people they want to get rid of, but I'm not interested in that. This is going to be a position of trust,

and I want each of you to help me build this system. I'm going to give you authority. I'm going to assume you're the best people in the country to work on this." Jack paused a moment, then concluded. "And oh, I want you all to go to a paint store and decide what color you want your office to be."

This last directive, as it turned out, earned the Price Commission some of its most positive news coverage in those crucial early days. Reflecting Jack's business beliefs as it surely does, the choice of paint color also produced a staff that grew to 600 before Phase II ended, each man or woman working long hours even though there was no clock to punch. Clocks, quite simply, didn't fit in with Jack's color scheme. "It became a high-morale operation," he says. "The people were trusted to make the best decisions they could make. And I got as many levels of bureaucracy out of there as possible."

Of all the raids for staff Jack conducted, the numerous marriages of bureaucratic convenience to get his organization up and running fast, no relationship attracted more comment than his eventual partners in investigation and enforcement. Jack didn't end up working back at the FBI. The perfect people for checking a company's books ended up being the Internal Revenue Service. The act of a business seeking a price increase involved showing the commission all its numbers and precisely how those numbers were derived. This would be as simple as Accounting 101, if presented openly and honestly. But naturally, these numbers weren't always presented that way. One company that asked for an increase kept brushing aside requests for its detailed bookkeeping on grounds it didn't have access to accountants who were that sophisticated. Don't worry, the commission replied, the IRS has plenty of sophisticated accountants who'd be more than happy to go over the books. The company dropped its application and never submitted another. As one journalist wrote at the time, "The IRS, like a seven-foot center in basketball, may be effective just by being there."

During the very first two weeks, Jack called together one session with up to thirty respected economists from places like Harvard,

Yale, Dartmouth and Chicago, asking them what they would do in his position. As expected, the answers ranged from keeping the price freeze in place indefinitely (not really an option) to "extract capitalist blood" (not really a goal). The man who ran the Price Commission during World War II advised Jack that the job ahead would require 16,000 or 17,000 employees (not really a possibility). A second, similar session gathered the chairmen of major corporations like IBM, GM and GE. Yes, Jack wanted to gain such knowledge as they were willing and able to offer, but first and foremost he wanted to earn their sympathy for the mind-numbing task ahead. He visited with Arthur Burns, head of the Federal Board. He visited with the head of the Council of Economic Advisors. He wanted them to know he was facing a problem almost no one could solve and that he was committed—as he was—to letting the muscles of free enterprise continue to do the heavy lifting. He wanted their ideas, but the best he got was "Do your best to preserve our free enterprise system."

Jack never did come to feel close to President Nixon, though the two did agree that he would come to the White House whenever he wanted or needed the President's ear. Their meetings were always cordial but brief and routine. Much, Jack sees now, was left unsaid by Nixon, who left the pressuring to Rumsfeld and Cheney. Jack became quite familiar with names that would later become infamous during the Watergate scandal. When those first news stories about a break-in at Democratic Party headquarters inside the Watergate Building started appearing in the media, Jack called Shultz to ask what was going on. "Stay out of this," came the brusque instruction from the man who'd recruited him. "You don't want to know. And you don't want to make any comments because you don't know anything." In the end, Shultz's advice made perfect sense, and Jack was glad he followed it.

Early on, in addition to increasingly regular news conferences, Jack was subjected to a comprehensive interview by Flora Lewis of *The New York Times*. Her assignment was not only to capture the day's headline, for a change, but also to profile the commission and

the tough job it had been given. The commission's PR person warned Jack that Lewis was tough: an excellent writer but well-prepared and unlikely to be charmed easily. Be careful what you say to her, Jack was warned. He was careful, but also candid, sharing his own feelings about the uncertainty of his position and the by-no-means guaranteed results. The result of the interview, along with visits Lewis paid to several other members of his team, may well be the most glowing review the Price Commission would ever receive in the media.

"Literally and bureaucratically, nobody has been here before," Lewis wrote, accurately. "The bleary-eyed people hurrying along the corridors may find their way, but they won't find the way things used to be done. Their very existence as a bureaucracy is a contradiction—their task is to make a competitive economy work by imposing restrictions, to release economic vitality by sitting on prices and wages." Elsewhere in the lengthy profile, Lewis observed that "Grayson's emergence as the key figure is based on his personality, his drive, his independent-mindedness, his firmness—he is the one who can make it work if it can be made to work at all."

In the beginning of the Price Commission's efforts, Jack felt himself welcomed to Washington by Rumsfeld and Cheney; and as a man living in a strange city away from his wife and children, he did enjoy the VIP treatment. He spent several evenings at dinner at Rumsfeld's house, getting to know the official and his wife. On another occasion, Rumsfeld and Cheney invited Jack to join them for a weekend of skeet shooting at the presidential retreat in Camp David, Maryland. As a country boy in ways neither of them could ever be, Jack remembers outshooting them. At a later date, they arranged for all members of the Price Commission to sail upriver to Mount Vernon aboard the presidential yacht.

In simplified terms, the Price Commission's job was to assess requests for price increases from businesses and then say Yes or No. There was no system, no model, in place when Jack went to work; to his dismay, he was simply told, "Create one." As a result, a company's request for a price increase was judged against a profit margin

during a base period several years earlier. As stated when he took the position, the goal was to slow national inflation as measured by the Consumer Price Index to two percent per year. Jack would indeed achieve it by the end of his tenure as chairman.

The position put Jack between the crosshairs of just about everybody inside and outside the Beltway. Consumers could and did complain that the prices of necessary things were going up faster than their paychecks. Business leaders could and did complain that their costs were going up, without the ability to raise prices to cover them. And, perhaps most surprisingly to this DC newcomer, the political system could and did complain that Jack was refusing to honor commitments its political candidate had made to this or that company, this or that wealthy executive or this or that special interest group, in return for support and campaign contributions.

In recalling his days in Washington, Jack often thinks of the naive but admirably straight-shooting Jimmy Stewart in *Mr. Smith Goes to Washington*. He learned a new term—"marker." A marker is like an IOU: "We have a marker out with the auto industry." Or "we have a marker out with the cattlemen." In other words, we owe them a favor, and we need to say yes to the higher prices they're asking for. Yet if Jack's mandate was to do something he didn't believe in to preserve America's economy, the last thing that made sense was letting approval go to the highest bidder. A collision course with the White House was set, long before Jack was savvy enough about the ways of DC to realize it. But no one ever interfered with these decisions from the White House or Rumsfeld or Cheney.

While huge, national news stories passed through Jack's department for days and weeks on end—steel prices, coal prices, automobile prices, food prices—more often than not the challenges seem almost humorous with hindsight. Some raw agricultural products were, for example, completely exempt from price control. If a shrimp boat in the Gulf of Mexico brought in shrimp with its nets, would the price of those raw shrimp be controlled by Jack's commission? And what if the same shrimp were frozen? If horse sperm were sold

Jack and Louis Neeb
speaking before Congress

Jack and the boys in DC

Washington, DC: 1971

frozen for breeding, would the Price Commission control that price? Yes, it turned out. But if two horses did what nature inspired them to, there would be no control of a raw agricultural product. In other words, the commission didn't control the price of peanuts, but it did mandate the price of peanut butter.

Prostitutes in Nevada, where the profession is legal, were asking to raise their prices. A very unofficial committee quickly formed to go out and conduct a "field experiment." As little official support developed for that research, the price increase was turned down.

So much proved to be at stake in price controls that Jack found himself being offered every conceivable kind of gift or bribe, primarily from lobbyists for huge corporations to keep deniability in place. Jack turned them all down if they did not comply with the regulations, and he ordered every member of his staff, from the highest to the lowest, to do the same. That meant turning down invitations to take someone's company jet to New York City for a night at the Metropolitan Opera, to be flown to Georgia for a weekend of quail hunting or to travel to a private-sector job when controls were over. As with the cost of granting favors requested by the White House, Jack understood instantly that if his commission's goodwill was for sale then its work meant worse than nothing.

Jack's handling of the requests for price increases from the automobile and coal industries stand out as testaments to the depth of his ethical conviction. The automakers in Detroit asked the Price Commission for an enormous increase, citing the upward spiral of their costs. This was a hot-button issue, since automakers and their

Oval Office: Donald Rumsfeld, George Boldt, Jack, President Richard Nixon

unionized workers represented millions of votes in any national election, not to mention one of the legacy industries of the still-stressed US economy. In fact, the automakers were so confident of their request that they had already sent the new prices to the dealerships, where they were being advertised. The trouble was the new prices violated guidelines that the Price Commission had firmly put in place. Jack had to say no, forcing the companies to roll back their increases. He even phoned John Connally, the former Texas governor now serving as chairman of the Cost of Living Council, to warn him what was about to happen.

"I hope you know what you're doing," Connally said.

"I do."

The Price Commission said no to Detroit, forcing the automakers to back away from price increases already announced. To their credit, at least for making the best of a bad situation, most took to advertising their forced generosity as an act of pure-hearted patriotism. With car prices substantially lower on lots across America, the automakers ended with a record year of new-car sales. "I gave them a lesson in capitalism," Jack laughs. "And they thanked me for it later."

Equally tense was the standoff between the Price Commission and the coal industry, which tied its request for a price increase to a threat that, without one, Americans in the northern states might freeze during their long, hard winter. Increasingly, this was the kind of request Jack was seeing on his desk: White House friends seeking price relief by painting a dire picture of the alternative. And the idea of people dying in the icy darkness always generates a few headlines, especially in the North. The coal industry had managed to pass an increased wage package through Nixon's Pay Board, led by George Boldt, giving the miners led by George Meany of the AFL-CIO a pay raise of eight percent. This, they argued, should be passed on to consumers, since the federal government's own Pay Board had given its approval.

This decision involved not only the relationship of government to business but also that between one government agency and another. To Jack, however, there was only one defensible stance: the Pay Board could decide whatever it thought best but the Price Commission had to remain independent. It had to use its own calculations and its own judgment, essentially ignoring the political consequences, and do what made sense for the economy. A rise in the price of coal would be inflationary well beyond the acceptable two percent, and Jack told the coal industry they'd have to live with the increases they'd been given and improve their productivity. The Pay Board's approval had no bearing, Jack declared. As a result of this stand, Arthur Burns, the chairman of the Federal Reserve Board, later declared the coal decision "our finest hour."

In a move that seems familiar within the early twenty-first century's healthcare debate, Blue Cross Blue Shield sought an increase in its premiums that included a threat that tens of thousands of American might lose coverage altogether if the answer was no. The answer was indeed no. "You do what you have to do," Jack remembers telling Blue Cross, a phrase that had entered his vocabulary in a major way by now. "I'm not trying to hurt health insurance. I'm trying to provide price controls."

The same kind of forces came into play during a brief but highly publicized flap with US Agriculture Secretary Earl Butz. A figure with more color than tact, Butz gave a speech about farmers being the backbone of American life and deserving an increase in farm prices to keep up with inflation. He accused Jack Grayson personally of hurting the agricultural industry, a charge that stung since the chairman had grown up on a farm and had even been a farmer himself. Jack was giving a speech that same day, so he wrote in a paragraph informing Butz that he wasn't about to back away from enforcing the commission's clear guidelines about price increases. As soon as the speech was over, a *New York Times* reporter raced up to ask Jack, "Did you clear that with the White House?"

"No," Jack replied.

Jack got a headline with that one, inspiring Rumsfeld to call on behalf of the President the next day and suggest he and Butz stop arguing in public. They did. Jack suspects that Butz was given the same message.

Another flap, presumably tongue-in-cheek for all concerned, placed Jack in disagreement with the AFL-CIO's same George Meany, based on a statement he made in pursuit of higher wages for members of his union. Implying that the Price Commission was failing to do its job, Meany charged that the makers of canned matzo ball soup were essentially raising prices by cutting the number of matzo balls in each can from four to three. When he heard of Meany's remarks—and knowing that George Meany was seldom wrong—Jack asked his staff about the matter, and no one knew anything. He formed teams to go from store to store throughout Washington and northern Virginia, buying and bringing back as many as seventy-five cans. The cans were opened at the office, the number of matzo balls dutifully counted. Jack was going on *Face the Nation* that weekend and with his best country-boy grin in place, he informed Meany via national television that he was mistaken. Jack even smuggled a can of Mrs. Adler's soup into the studio, hid it beside his chair and finally pulled it out at the proper moment to show to the cameras, "just for drama," he admits now.

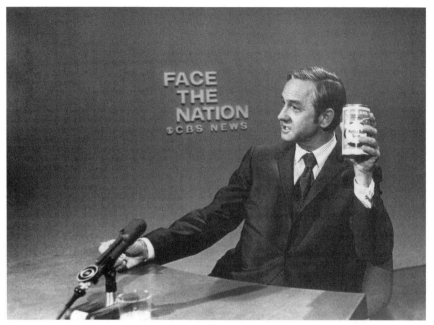

Face the Nation: 1972

As an opponent of federal price controls before accepting the job of administering them, Jack always saw the policy as a short-term solution to a specific inflationary problem—not as a way to govern America. He always thought of Phase II as a step away from the price freeze of Phase I toward an economy that ran on the muscle of free enterprise. He certainly hoped that, in the same voice he'd use to discuss price controls with news media, he could someday detail their complete dismantling. Thanks as usual to White House politics, Jack was never able to give that speech.

The situation at the Price Commission was untenable. Through one of the policies put in place as a political compromise, companies whose requests had been turned down were allowed to file for exceptions. This was not so much a legal appeal using the same facts as an assertion of different facts: we've changed the beef stew and need a price increase, we've altered the dress and need a price increase, etc. Jack went to Rumsfeld and told him that, if businesses were resorting to such extreme measures to sneak around price controls, the controls

were now doing more harm than good. The Price Commission, Jack said, would need more staff to deal with this mountain of exceptions. Or else the government should get out of the price control business, which was what Jack recommended. Either way, he told Rumsfeld, he felt his work was done and he would be resigning from the Commission.

What Nixon and his advisers decided to do, in Phase III, struck Jack as the worst of both worlds. It essentially divided sectors of the economy into two different lists, one remaining under price controls and the other liberated from them. Jack thought this was a terrible decision and tendered his resignation to the President almost immediately. In order to not imply a disagreement, he said his phase of price controls had simply reached its goal and that he was proud of the way the American economy had responded.

Nixon, Rumsfeld and company accepted Jack's resignation, predictably, but did ask him to stay on, mostly to keep up the appearances of a smooth transition, for another couple months. Jack agreed, bringing Barbara and the kids from San Miguel to enjoy some time without work in the nation's capital and also some downtime at the farm. They rented a small house in the tiny section of Chevy Chase that slipped over into the District from Maryland. It was time for Jack to ponder the meaning of all he'd done here—as well as to wonder what he was supposed to do next.

His position as dean of the SMU Business School was still there and waiting. And other offers came his way. John Connally called Jack about possibly serving as Secretary of Commerce; but considering what he'd just been through, it was easy for Jack to say no. Influential Republican Anne Armstrong called to ask him to chair the national Bicentennial celebration being planned for 1976, but Jack turned that down too. He did have to smile later when the man who did chair the Bicentennial, John Warner of Virginia, ended up marrying Elizabeth Taylor. Maybe Liz, Jack quipped, had come with the deal somehow.

If jobs didn't excite him during these two months, writing about

The boys at the farm

Randy, Michael

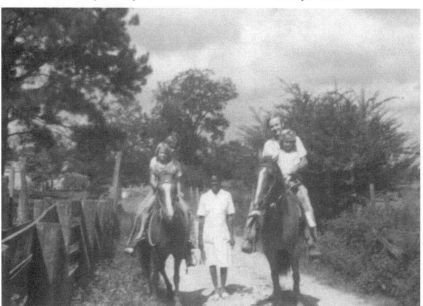

Right to left: Michael, Louella, Randy with Jack on the farm

his time as chairman did. He produced several articles about his thoughts on price controls—consistent thoughts over many years, now deepened by personal experience. One of the articles, called "Let's Get Back to the Competitive Market System," won a Harvard Business School McKinsey Award as the top business article of that year. This encouraged Jack to turn his experiences into a full-length

Confessions of a Price Controller

book titled *Confessions of a Price Controller*, published in 1974 by Dow Jones-Irwin and written with the man who perhaps had done the most to help get the commission up and running, Louis Neeb. Not surprisingly, as the tale neared its end, Jack embarked on an impassioned (and wildly detailed) defense of a free enterprise system he saw increasingly threatened by a national attitude that accepted high levels of government intervention.

Drawing on history going back to Diocletian of Rome in 301 CE, and including Kublai Khan in the thirteenth century, Jack outlines the three major reasons he supports an economy based on markets over any other the world has ever seen. The first is "demonstrated economic superiority," based on America producing the highest standard of living in history and demonstrating the most remarkable ability to adapt to changing conditions. Nothing else had worked in forty centuries. The second, he says, is "personal freedom"—always a condition close to Jack's heart. The principles of democracy and personal freedom,

quite simply, exist most comfortably within a free-market economy, he argues. As a third reason, he offers his own then-recent experience trying to control prices. It is impossible, he argues, for such regulation to improve on a system in which the public determines the allocation of resources by a "billion daily market decisions."

"The growth in the public's disenchantment with the private enterprise system has been matched by the public's demand on that system," Jack writes near the end of *Confessions*. "The public wants, for instance, higher pay for teachers, police and women; a clean environment; better schools and medical care—and all without increases in prices or taxes." And, a few pages later:

> "I am not saying, however, that the private enterprise system is doomed, nor that continuance of the trend toward central control is inevitable and irreversible. Nor do I feel that government has no role in the economic allocation system. It clearly does and should. I believe, rather, that we are very near the point where further centralization will change our present system into one that can no longer perform its function efficiently. I view this trend with alarm because I favor retaining the very powerful features of the market system."

The only answer to this conundrum—the public's loss of faith in a system from which it continues to demand more—is contained in the single word Jack Grayson found himself using with increasing frequency: productivity. America was falling behind in the productivity race, he had come to believe, as well as in the pursuit of a broad array of things he called simply "quality." Many of the nation's overseas competitors were actively, specifically and aggressively pursuing both, even as the heads of major American corporations seemed to understand little about how to improve either of them. A center should be founded, Jack proclaimed at the end of *Confessions*, as well as in a speech to the Economics Club of Detroit and in a *Business Week* editorial published July 14, 1973, titled "How to

Make Productivity Grow Faster"—a center for American productivity and quality, embracing a far-reaching mission of researching it, teaching it, preaching it and proving that it *can* happen here, against what seemed dizzying odds. "I submit that it is already late in time to get such an Institute organized, funded and developed," Jack wrote in the magazine editorial. "I submit that it is a private sector responsibility to bring such an Institute into existence."

"Two weeks after that piece appeared," Jack remembers, "the editor of *Business Week* called and told me nobody was working to start such a group. 'Jack,' the editor said, 'how about you?'"

14

BIRTH OF A NOTION

FOR ALMOST TWO YEARS, JACK AND BARBARA had been effectively separated, Jack being immersed in price controls in DC and Barbara focused on her art and the children in Mexico. When they got back together in DC, it took only a short time before each realized the marriage was not working. They agreed to separate amicably, were divorced, and she took the children. The two are still good friends today. When Jack got back to SMU and his office, it was not long before he fell in love with Cynthia Daniel, a secretary at the business school. He ended up marrying her.

As Jack settled back into campus life, he called upon his high level contacts from DC to visit the University as speakers, donors and supporters. Jack even asked President Ford, who had now replaced Nixon, to speak at a conference for alumni and business leaders. The event was a sellout with more than 2000 attendees.

Even though Jack was now still the dean of the business school as had been the understanding before he embarked to DC, his worldview was now national and international. He was still thinking about what he had learned as price control czar about a business' failure to pay attention to productivity and quality and the imminent decline of competitiveness with the world, especially with Japan, if the US did not change. He applauded Edwards Deming (the quality guru who had restored Japan's competitiveness) with a focus on quality and productivity and agreed wholeheartedly with the scholar's

SMU conference with President Ford

documentary of that time titled "If Japan Can, Why Can't We?"

Jack was asked to join a government sponsored and funded National Commission on Productivity. He declined, believing all it would produce were more articles, more meetings, more discussions and no action. It died after a year or so.

He had one more shot of getting the nation to focus on productivity. President Ford asked him to come to Washington and work with Paul McCracken, a well-known University of Michigan economist, to prepare for the President a productivity program for the nation. That proposition excited Jack, for he knew McCracken also believed in productivity as a source for national economic growth. Here was a chance to recommend what the nation needed to do to re-start its competitive engines. Jack asked to bring along Bobby Lyle and a secretary from SMU, and they spent two weeks in the Old Executive Office building and prepared a proposed national program on productivity.

On the very day they were prepared to present it to the President, Bill Seidman—Ford's chief of staff—came into the room and said, "I'm sorry, but the President listened to someone else and has decided not to use your program and instead use a program called WIN." "What in the hell is WIN?!" the group asked with dismay. They were told, "It's Whip Inflation Now."

"The White House is going to organize meetings across the nation to listen to ideas from the public on how to reduce inflation. We will get leading speakers, organize discussion groups in major cities and universities and distribute thousands of WIN buttons that citizens can wear to show their support."

"Idiotic!" was Jack's response. "That's the craziest idea I've ever heard!" But Seidman said, "Sorry, that's what the President wants to do, and he's the President." So, the group discarded its program, folded up its tents and went home. "I still have a WIN button buried deep somewhere," Jack says. In that moment, however, he decided he wanted no more government-sponsored efforts to improve productivity and quality. His dream had to be created, funded, operated and managed by the private sector.

Jack resigned his position at SMU as dean of the business school, taking on the task of restoring America's competitiveness through more emphasis on productivity for and by the private sector. He knew that it would take money—big time money—so he decided to set up a fundraising operation to form a new organization to wake up American business. He created a corporation in 1975, with two friends of his at SMU as witnesses, called the American Productivity Center and applied for a 501(c)3 tax exemption. Jack felt the nonprofit avenue promised the greatest degree of freedom, not only in terms of mission but also in terms of fundraising, which he knew he would need. As yet he had no money, nor any clear idea as to how he was going to get it.

Getting an office with a phone was the easy part. The retailer J.C. Penney had a building in Dallas and gave Jack permission to use office space there for the gargantuan sales job he knew he was embarking upon. Building what he had in mind—whether the Executive Renewal Center as first envisioned, or the American Productivity Center (APC) as it launched, or the eventual APQC as it is known now—would require some serious money. What's worse is that, having tapped the Dallas business community several times for funding for SMU, Jack decided he couldn't go back to the locals. His support would have

to come from someone else, somewhere else, presumably from the major corporations he had dealt with in various ways while chairing the Price Commission. Jack settled into his borrowed office space and started writing hundreds of letters. And as any teacher knows going in, the more times and ways he described his vision in writing, the better he understood exactly what he was trying to achieve.

The network he built in Washington would be extremely valuable to his new adventure. Using these contacts, he was able to get in the door in some very high places, setting his ideas for a productivity center designed to help American businesses in competitiveness and the newly emerging global economy before the heads of corporations like Ford, GE, IBM and the World Bank, all before "making the ask" for what he then estimated would be $39 million. His pitch was generally well received. In one beneficial coincidence, Jack was invited to speak at a conference in Hawaii by the leadership of IBM. As soon as Jack's talk ended, the corporation's No. 2 issued some standard business pleasantry like, "And Jack, if there's ever anything we can help you with, we hope you won't hesitate to call." In his recollection, shortly after Jack dragged the unsuspecting executive back to his hotel room and told him more than he ever wanted to know about productivity and quality. IBM pledged one million dollars in fairly short order. The pledge had one caveat; it was dependent on Jack's financial goals for the project being met. IBM wasn't willing to provide their million unless Jack could deliver funding that would allow him to achieve the vision. That fine print set in motion the first great threat to APC ever happening.

Jack, after all, used the IBM offer as a talking point each time he met with or called a business decision maker, implying that person should follow the smart money. Yet when the projected fundraising timeframe had elapsed without the projected level of success, Jack received a letter from IBM Chairman Frank Cary saying that the deal was off. As several pledges from other companies were predicated on IBM support, this change of heart jeopardized everything. Jack picked up the phone. Cary insisted he was sorry but that was the

agreement, and Jack explained, almost begging, that IBM needed to reconsider since the whole effort might fall apart otherwise. Cary said he was sorry again, but there was really nothing he could do.

"May I come talk with you?" Jack asked.

"My schedule is packed, as always," responded the chairman. "Maybe in a month or two."

"Frank, I can't wait that long. What about this week? Next week?"

"Next week I'm giving a speech at the Plaza in New York. But I won't have time to see you."

"You're going to wear a tux, right? For your speech? Where are you going to dress?"

"In my room."

"Well, okay. I'll come to New York and stay out of your way while you're dressing. But at least I'll get a chance to change your mind."

With considerable reluctance, Cary agreed to Jack's unusual request. And Jack flew immediately to New York, went to the Plaza Hotel overlooking Central Park and talked to the chairman of IBM while he was busy inserting cufflinks and straightening his bowtie. As a result, IBM renewed its offer of a million dollars for APC, with a $200,000 donation upfront and the rest due in increments after that. To this day, Jack keeps two letters in a frame side by side in his office: the first one canceling the IBM support and the second reinstating it. They remind him how many extra miles a person needs to travel to make his dream come true.

In addition to the IBM support, other large donations in those early years included one million dollars from The Pew Charitable Trusts, $500,000 from the Potlatch Corporation and $500,000 from Weyerhaeuser. The remainder of support primarily came in increments of $50,000 to $100,000.

Every effective sales pitch needs a story, and, increasingly each time he told it, the story Jack carried in his briefcase was one that was crucial to America. It was based on theories and research, to be sure,

going back to his days as a business school dean. But the story was even more impacted by the fifteen months he spent chairing the Price Commission. Time after time, he had asked American corporations for their measurements of productivity and quality, and they insisted they didn't keep their books that way. Eventually, he came to believe their answer, and it was sobering. He knew from his academic work that such measurements, and the centers to help companies make them, already existed in Japan and Germany, part of the recovery funded with American dollars as part of the Marshall Plan. Other European countries, including France and the Netherlands, had committed significant funding to researching productivity and quality as a method of improving their financial standing.

Yet the world's strongest economy, the victor of all victors in that same war, professed to know little about productivity and simply relied on improving market share, earnings per share, stock price and customer satisfaction—all outcomes, not productivity, quality or efficiency. He wondered how this could be possible that the leaders within the largest companies in America failed to understand what drove productivity inside the very companies where they sat at the helm. Jack felt certain all this had to change and change quickly. If his native land was to continue to be the leader in world competitiveness, they simply must understand productivity and quality.

He knew a definition of productivity from his days of studying and later teaching economics. It was output divided by input, a measure of how much return you got on whatever you put in. That sounded easy, but only in a classroom. America's best and brightest companies had difficulty coming up with even the right numbers to divide. Even without any numbers to prove it, however, Jack was convinced that US productivity had slumped, especially by comparison with the revived economies of our former enemies. And all the business leaders he talked to could do was blame organized labor, and all organized labor could do was blame cheap imports. There was more to the equation than that, Jack knew. And the blaming wasn't getting the country anywhere.

"So what went wrong?" Jack was asked by virtually everyone he asked for money. "What went wrong and how do you plan to fix it?" Most of these people knew Jack from the Price Commission and therefore were ready to grant him some credibility. But they weren't necessarily ready to abandon all the usual whipping boys and consider whether at least some of the fault might lie within themselves.

As for a set of basic mistakes, Jack had to look no farther than his recent time in the federal government. He certainly pointed to the "kind, amount and speed" of government intervention in business, the same forces he'd cited in business articles after leaving the Nixon administration. As the inflation he'd battled at the Price Commission had its way with the economy, businesses and individuals found themselves in higher and higher tax brackets, thus losing more of their wealth to taxation. What's more, while regulation continued to correct some of the excesses that had caused trouble, it had tipped the balance too far, hurting the country's ability to produce goods and services in the market. The productivity of the government itself was an issue too, especially as it affected as much as a third of the gross national product. Both private industry and government suffered from a lack of understanding of what productivity was and how to understand performance around it. You can't fix what you don't understand. Jack knew that without change the United States markets would not be able to compete, and this was just the calm before the storm.

Still, Jack was not anti-government, since all the blame did not reside there. The private sector, he insisted from personal experience, had not paid enough attention to productivity and quality in recent years, even beginning to take both for granted. The juggernaut that had been America was slowing down.

"Unless the whole country pays attention to greater productivity," Jack warned in one interview, "we simply won't survive. That's the only way we're going to get inflation down, and that's the only way organizations are going to be truly efficient and effective at whatever it is they want to do."

Increasingly, despite denials from American automakers and other manufacturing concerns, postwar Japan seemed to be the problem—except that Jack decided, especially after travel and study, that Japan offered the solution. During the time he was working to fund APC, the Japanese auto industry went from a negligible five percent of the US market to upwards of twenty percent. By then the heads of Ford, GM and Chrysler weren't laughing anymore. After all it wasn't productivity they paid attention to, it was market share and that was showing a steep decline. The key, Jack came to believe, lay in studying the Japanese methods, many learned from American academic Edwards Deming. In spite of Deming's advice being rejected at home, the Japanese had taken stock and were using Deming's methods to focus their efforts on productivity and quality. As a result they were winning in the American market share race.

On the home front, instead of management and labor blaming each other, they'd have to work together or both ends of the spectrum would be unemployed. They had to study and internalize the Japanese concepts of quality, quality circles, *kaizen* (defined as improvement, change for the best), *kanban* (developed at Toyota, a system for lean, just-in-time production) and especially the empowerment of employees to "stop the line" whenever they spotted a defect or problem. As unthinkable as it would be in hierarchy-obsessed America, if the lowest Japanese worker spotted a problem with a product, he could shout, "Stop the line!" The empowerment of such a system impressed Jack beyond measure, years before empowerment became a standard-issue phrase in American business.

US businessmen still clung to their notion of invincibility, rejecting the changes Jack was recommending because they didn't make money. Some, however, did join Jack, some academics, and even some labor officials for a tour of Japanese factories, underwritten by Westinghouse with a $250,000 donation. The tour was not only Toyota for cars but Sony for electronics and even Kikkoman for soy sauce. What they witnessed, despite the dramatic language and

cultural barriers, was a quest for productivity and quality that never ends. What they saw was businesses run simultaneously from "the top down and the bottom up." What they saw, Jack would argue, was the future of business.

"I wish," said one US auto executive touring a Japanese assembly line, "we had people like this back in Flint."

"The tragedy," replied one of the workers in perfect English, "is that you do."

As Jack noted during this and other tours, the Japanese had made a national commitment to productivity improvement in every sector of their economy: profit, nonprofit, labor union and government. They were investing heavily in capital equipment, a much higher percentage of their gross national product than was found in the United States, with the result that their factories were modern, highly automated and extremely efficient. The Japanese, he observed, had long-term goals in business, whereas his own countrymen had short-term objectives.

Not surprisingly, Jack was fascinated by experimentation, especially when it spoke to the heart of his mission and message. In Sweden, for instance, a group of auto workers who'd spent years building a single small part of each car were allowed to build an entire auto, with a resulting increase in productivity brought on by their sense of personal investment and accomplishment. In Japan, teams of workers were inspired to work together, exercise together and even sing together. And again, the result was measurably greater productivity. Everywhere he turned there were lessons to be learned, all causing Jack to have greater hope for the American worker if he could be properly focused on the task.

In Fremont, California, he recounted, at a GM plant producing cars, productivity was low, morale was poor and the business was about to go broke—until Toyota bought a fifty percent share and started to run the place. The same workers stayed on under Japanese managers, who introduced their methods, ideas and relationships. The plant became one of the finest and fastest in the United States using Japanese methods. Little did Jack know that these tours around

Fundraising

the globe, being used to open the eyes of American businessmen to the possibilities of productivity and quality, were the birth of what would later become a widely used management tool known as best practice site visits. They would remain at the heart of APC's, and later APQC's, research on any question, any situation, any problem.

Throughout the mid 1970s, with gospel and hat in hand, Jack met with business after business seeking funding for APC. He carried a projector wherever he went so he could give a slide show, and eventually, he carried a bell. It was a gift from IBM on the day they handed him that first check, and it has stayed with Jack ever since. APQC rings the bell to this day each time it signs up a new member. Many who remember Jack during his quest for early APC funding said, "You didn't want to sit next to Jack at dinner," as those who did found themselves in an argument they couldn't win and ultimately signed up to help fund an American Productivity Center.

In its earliest iteration, mapped out shortly after Jack left SMU, the place he had in mind was to be called the Executive Renewal Center, and it was to be built in Dallas. Jack envisioned a facility that would be part 150-room hotel, part conference center, part fitness

center and spa and part business think tank, available to companies and individuals for conferences, seminars and workshops, medical examinations, exercise programs, personal renewal and recreation. From his studies of Japan, Jack had taken to heart the emphasis on physical fitness as a key to long-term productivity. The center he wanted to build, he put it confidently, "will be unique in the world."

Not surprisingly, with his plan's emphasis on what a later generation would call wellness, Jack made the acquaintance of Dr. Kenneth Cooper of Dallas. Creator of the famous aerobics concept and author of several best-selling books on the subject, Cooper already had 900 executive members of his health club, with many more high-profile business leaders coming to Dallas for check-ups. The way Jack saw it, he and Cooper could be natural partners, with the Executive Renewal Center rising from unused acreage that was part of Cooper Clinic and serving as a natural draw for national and international clientele. Initially, Cooper expressed interest in Jack's proposal, which at that time carried a price tag of just under $11.9 million. But, according to Jack, Cooper eventually realized what a large commitment would be required of him as essentially a real estate developer and opted instead to focus on his medical practice. Jack was, despite friends in high places, on the street once again.

Cooper did, at Jack's request, put him in touch with someone he thought might be interested—Tom Fatjo, chairman of Browning-Ferris Industries (BFI), who agreed to fly up from Houston for a meeting. The two men found themselves to be kindred spirits, with Tom's success building BFI from a waste company with a single truck into a national concern perfectly reflecting Jack's more theoretical belief in entrepreneurship. In one of life's supreme ironies, BFI had also been the first company Jack had cited for violating price controls, his decision coming just as BFI was courting Wall Street with an eye toward going public. BFI had hurried to Washington to appeal to Jack personally, but all he could tell them was to lower their prices. They did, in near-record time, with as little attention paid as possible. Now the two principals from that confrontation were talking about

creating something huge, ambitious and a tad vague together, with the accompanying need for trust.

The two talked about every aspect of the Executive Renewal Center, and Tom agreed with nearly all the ideas Jack had been forming for years as an academic and as a government official. The only requirement he set down to make his participation a reality was that the center had to be built in Houston. Not Dallas.

Jack confessed to knowing little or nothing about the larger Texas city on the Gulf Coast, which had achieved varying degrees of fame throughout the twentieth century when oil was discovered at nearby Spindletop, when the Houston Ship Channel connected its port to the world and when President Lyndon Johnson chose it as home for the space program's Mission Control. Like Dallas, Houston was a city of go-getters, which Jack knew he would like. But he also envisioned it as a place already filled with buildings, not exactly the lovely setting he had imagined gazing at Ken Cooper's open land beside a lake. Tom invited Jack to come down for a visit and almost immediately put him in a car and drove him to the place he already had in mind.

In the mid-1970s, the plot of land, in a corner created by Interstate 10 and Loop 610 north of the Galleria shopping mall, was to Jack nothing less than an oasis. It was the kind of place you could stand and forget you were in the middle of a great, loud and bustling business city, which was exactly what Jack wanted. There were mansions built on the land, with only a handful of wealthy families enjoying precisely these attributes. There was a challenge, Tom explained, in addition to simply raising enough money to buy people out. There was a common deed restriction declaring that no resident could sell without the approval of all the others. Jack was already $8000 in debt personally, so he figured what could be the harm of talking to millionaires living in mansions about buying them out.

Jack and Tom met with homeowners individually, telling them of their plans for a center with a top-flight hotel, conference venue and spa and listening carefully to the homeowners' concerns. There was an opportunity within those deed restrictions that would prove

Business Week Article: Houstonian

crucial to their eventual success. The same restrictions that made it difficult for the two men made it difficult for homeowners to ever sell. That became key to all selling, no matter whatever personally motivated the owners—the good of the country, the cash for their land or simply because if they didn't, they might not get another opportunity. Here were two men with professional respect, a certain amount of financial backing and a vision the community might rally around. In the end, Jack and Tom were able to acquire twenty acres, just enough, along with the permission of all the residents. And they got the land for something less than they'd have had to pay for similar acreage on the open market.

By this point, Jack was moving away from the name Executive Renewal Center for something quite different—the Foundation for Business, Politics and Economics. The new name made sense, he reasoned, since he had seen in Washington how much politics had to do with business and economics. And calling it a foundation fit in with his idea that the entire development would be built as a nonprofit organization. That, like the new name that never caught on, was about to change dramatically.

Jack and Tom scheduled a meeting in downtown Houston to show leaders in the local business community—oil company executives, bankers and wealthy individuals—what they were seeking to create. They had an architect build a model of the center and set about, once their guests were settled in, explaining why they needed upwards of $25 million. And there the meeting ground to a halt. There was no

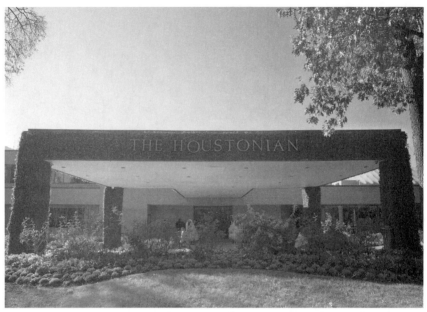

The Houstonian in 2014

way, they were told, that anybody would lend that amount of money to a nonprofit. "Nobody wants to foreclose on a nonprofit," one banker told them with extreme finality. "It looks bad."

Only after the meeting was breaking up, and the two presenters feeling their efforts were not going to produce, did an oil company executive draw them aside to make a suggestion. What if their foundation was created as a nonprofit to raise money for an APC building, he said, but the rest of the campus was built for profit? That way the hotel, conference center, spa and proposed restaurants could operate as regular businesses, which bankers could understand and assess on their fiscal merits, while the foundation could be left out of the profit equation. In the interest of finding its way to life, the foundation had to divorce itself from the operations of the glistening facility next door—Jack remaining in charge of APC and Tom of the hotel complex—while still remaining joined physically. That facility went on to achieve success in the hospitality industry, ultimately becoming one of the premier hotels and spas in Houston, The Houstonian

Fundraising

Hotel, Club and Spa. In one of history's nicer touches, Gay Roane, whose family owned one of the original homes purchased to make room for APC, later bought the hotel and resort via her company called Redstone and operates it to this day.

In addition, Jack and Tom wanted to live on the site. But that would take up extremely valuable space, so they decided to find a developer to build a new high rise condominium, adjoining the twenty-acre Houstonian property, so they and others could live there.

For APC's startup, Jack had raised $10 million to operate for the first five years, plus an additional five million dollars to design and construct an appropriate headquarters. Sometimes the donations took strange twists and turns. One wealthy individual agreed to donate $50,000 toward creating the productivity center, only to have the staff write the check for $500,000. As Jack remembers it, the lady fired that staff member but let him keep the check.

The nearly hundred original contributors, whose gifts were received prior to 1979, were designated as Founders. They span the alphabet from AMAX Foundation to Weyerhaeuser Company. Other familiar names, at least in their 1979 incarnations, include M.D. Anderson Foundation, Anheuser-Busch, Conoco, Corning Glass, Exxon, Ford, General Electric, General Foods, General Mills and General Motors, Gulf Oil, Heinz, Honeywell, Hughes Tool, Kaiser Aluminum, Memorex, Motorola, Price Waterhouse, Quaker Oats, Shell Oil, Southern Pacific, US Steel, Wells Fargo and Westinghouse. These names can still be seen, hand-carved into the acrylic in the lobby of APQC. In addition to corporate funding, APC also offered individual memberships, priced from ninety-nine to $150 per year, to access APC's library, research reports and publications.

Concurrent with the fundraising, Jack was actively recruiting and building APC's first board of directors with a specific goal to bring together all sectors of the economy. Sixty individuals joined the original board. Of those, twenty-three were sitting CEOs or chairmen, nine were heads of national unions and ten were members of higher education institutions. Some of the more widely known members at that time included Tom Peters, Rosabeth Moss Kantor, John Connally, Ed Lawler, Pierre DuPont and Bill Usery.

During this time Jack came to be acquainted with lawyer Joe Jaworski. Joe's father Leon was a prominent attorney in Houston and a Nixon prosecutor. Tom Fatjo knew the family and the foundation that Leon ran would be a potential fit for their project, so Jack and Tom created a presentation to request $500,000. They secured the funding and also Joe, who joined their efforts to develop and run the successful Leadership Program within The Houstonian, a companion program to APC focused on developing leaders. The program ultimately expanded to more than a dozen cities over the years.

As early as 1976, Jack pulled together a list of seven major objectives for what would become the American Productivity Center. These would evolve over the years but never wander far from the founder's original vision. The center was designed to create awareness

of "productivity and the quality of working life" through articles, speeches and videos. To serve as a one-stop information resource for companies and individuals wrestling with what was becoming an increasing problem in the American economy, the center would conduct research and develop a series of appraisal and measurement techniques to be used by governments and businesses as well as develop a series of programs and support materials to help the effort along. It would "collect, develop, evaluate and disseminate" specific productivity improvement techniques. And, in one of APC's most intriguing calls-to-arms, it would work to achieve cooperation between labor and management. The group would, according to this objective, "foster a climate in which these traditional adversaries can work more effectively together to improve productivity and the quality of working life."

Time was also of the essence. Jack and Tom understood that if they entered the usual design procedure for their buildings, that portion of the job might take nine months, even a year, with revisions going back and forth by courier or mail. Intrigued by the French tradition of the *charrette*, based on the French word for "cart" or "chariot," Jack invited everyone involved in the design and building to the house he was living in on the site—and told them nobody left until they were in agreement. This, he remembers, took three days, with men sleeping in shifts and waking each other up to discuss troubling details. By 1976, as America settled in to celebrate the

Original drawing of the center

Bicentennial, Jack was ready to send his lead architect a remarkable memo about the headquarters in his dreams.

"I don't want you to think of this building as just steel, cement, square feet or a fixed, inanimate structure," he wrote to architect Philip Clifford Ewald. "It's human. Alive. When you walk in, you feel the humanity. You're excited—something's happening here. Fun. Creativity. Unexpected. It thinks human, it feels human. It is human." Jack exalted in things

APQC Hat Wall

that visitors to his headquarters would notice and appreciate forever more. "It thrives on beauty. It speaks with the language of art, suspense, whimsy... Surprise. Pushes your own renewal. It challenges you. It likes you and others around you. It likes teams, it facilitates communication, involvement, participation. It wants to help you realize your dreams. Your own life."

From the start, Jack followed a basic design he had scribbled into one of his notebooks while at SMU, borrowing and usually improving upon ideas he'd seen in corporate headquarters as far back as his time in Europe and at the Price Commission. There would

be, he decreed, no closed offices—simply desks arrayed throughout an open work area so workers could communicate easily with each other. Despite his own No. 1 role at APC, his desk was there too, so anybody could tell him or ask him anything in the course of a day. Other creative self-expressions made their way into APC's public areas, including a "hat wall" comprised of fifty-four different bits of headwear to show a wide variety of occupations and roles people play (a policeman, a nurse, a fireman, a Catholic cardinal, plus a fez from North Africa) and even a reproduced cuneiform from 2300 B.C. in Sumeria. Jack delights in pointing out to visitors that this was the earliest known written expression of his favorite word: freedom.

As the American Productivity Center came together, corporations that helped support it with cash also helped with personnel. Many sent individuals or even small teams of employees to Houston, a process known in business as providing *secondments* to a startup to serve as "associates," keeping them on the company payroll. Generally they returned with glowing reports about how the operation was taking shape.

The Cuneiform, a symbol of freedom, etched into the walls of APQC

In some ways, to Jack, this was Price Commission Part II, cobbling together the necessary staff from anywhere he could find it—except with corporate America playing the role of the federal government. And since the eventual home of the agency was a construction site, they had to find office space in the neighborhood: first on a floor of the nearby Texan Building and finally, when the staff outgrew that, at the Marriott Hotel on the 610 Loop. Carl Thor, an experienced executive that Jack found with Andrew Clayton's Cheese Division in Brazil, joined Jack as APC's first vice president of measurement. Thor went on to become president and vice chair during his fifteen years with APC. Jack proudly points to Carl as an example of the kind of people who caught the productivity and quality fever and went on to make a major difference in the world of quality improvement. Today, Carl Thor proudly serves on APQC's Board of Directors, still

remaining active in the organization he helped to build.

In the building that emerged among the trees, between the start of construction on March 5, 1979, and formal dedication on April 21, 1980, Jack was realizing his own dreams as well.

Tom Fatjo and Jack Grayson at the Houstonian's Groundbreaking

Founders' Day: 1980

15

GROWING THE DREAM

I N THOSE HEADY DAYS OF SELF-CREATION—
when the American Productivity Center was still operating out
of the Marriott Hotel—Weyerhaeuser joined other corporations
in donating staffers to help as associates in Houston. The first man
to travel from the Pacific Northwest lumber giant came back in awe
of all he experienced around the organization. This, he reported,
was exactly what American business needed to compete with the
Japanese, the Germans and anybody else who might make a play for
the newly global market. One graduate student and part-time staffer
listening to the man's excited report listened extra carefully. At the
end of it, she told her bosses, "I want to go."

Carla O'Dell found the work of APC exciting on several levels.
For one thing, now in her thirties and working with Weyerhaeuser,
Carla was intrigued with the basic ideas associated with productiv-
ity—especially the all-important human ones. She was a graduate
of Stanford now working on her master's degree in psychology and
doing research in Weyerhaeuser's sawmill and particle board plants,
so the very idea of trying to change the ways and reasons Americans
worked was fascinating to her. Carla drove from Eugene, Oregon,
to Houston in her tiny Volkswagen. Initially Jack had backed away
from the idea of her joining the staff at APC, fearing she brought with
her the perspective of academia he had spent much of his adult life
avoiding. Other staffers, however, convinced him the young woman

was impressive and should stay. After some reservations on Jack's part, Carla found a position at APC.

Launching APC required every ounce of talent, brilliance, persuasion, time and energy that Jack could possess. Nothing was on his mind but making both APC and The Houstonian a success. Cynthia practically didn't see him for days, and his mind was always elsewhere. Cynthia had no involvement with the project and nothing to do in the house alone on The Houstonian grounds, and the situation eventually took its toll on their marriage. This was made doubly painful because she was pregnant with the son they would name Daniel, born in 1980. The problem was not their personal relationship, it was a lack of involvement in this time-consuming passion that Jack had. They decided that it was best if they separated and divorced. Cynthia moved back to Dallas. As with former wives with whom Jack remained as close as possible, he still maintains an amicable relationship with Cynthia.

Carla O'Dell, on the other hand, had a work ethic similar to Jack's, embracing the long hours and intense concentration demanded of any zealot. She was a bright star, Jack remembers, and slow to anger. Jack found himself falling in love with Carla and was happy to discover that the feeling was mutual. Carla left APC to complete her Ph.D. dissertation while Jack's marriage came to an end. Two years later, Jack and Carla were married on December 11, 1982, using their honeymoon as a chance to attend a behavioral conference on the West Coast. On their way back to Houston, Jack learned that President Reagan was about to announce a national conference on productivity. He put in a call to Treasury Secretary William Simon and said he wanted to be a part of it. Jack was asked to join President Reagan's National Productivity Advisory Committee in 1982. This effort would mark Jack's involvement with a fourth US President, having most recently served on President Carter's Commission for a National Agenda for the 80s.

"I knew that if we did it," recalls Jack, who ended up serving as the conference's co-chairman and thus putting APC even more on the

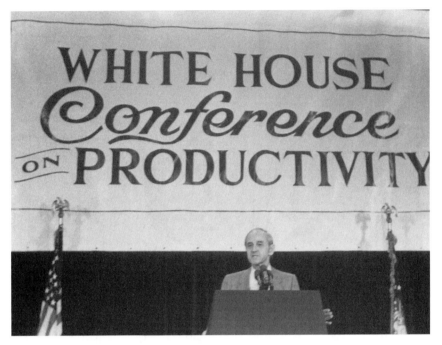

White House Conference on Productivity: 1982

national map, "we had to make it different from the typical White House conference. We couldn't be just another bunch of academics presenting papers only the authors cared about."

As usual, Jack and his minions succeeded in not being typical.

With his adept timing, Jack understood that if Japanese competition was the one thing American business leaders were talking about, computer technology was the main thing they weren't. And that technology, he knew, would be crucial to the future of American business. Plus, it was attention-getting. In preparation for his part of the White House conference, he traveled to New Jersey to arrange for use of bandwidth from GE, a time-shared computer system based in New Jersey, and then to California to solicit actual computers from the leadership of Apple. As he'd done with other donations in the past, Jack convinced the company that their Apple IIe would get a great deal of publicity if it played a starring role in a time-shared interactive computer conference of 175 business leaders from around

the nation talking around the clock about all that lay ahead. Apple donated 175 computers. When Jack finally did gather the leaders in the APC amphitheater in Houston, only about fifteen admitted having touched a keyboard. "My secretary handles all that," was the standard reply.

If the leaders were all supposed to stay in that room, Jack wouldn't have needed the computers. After introducing them to the project and its mission and dividing the 175 into seven groups with specific topics, he sent them home with their personal computers. It didn't take them long to be responding to each other at all hours of the day and night. For many involved in one of the world's first "computer conferences," 1983 had become the future.

Today, it's amusing to look at the typed-out pages of the group's final report, not least to see how words like "electronically" and "online" are kept in quotes, like words from a foreign language whose continent hasn't been discovered. But the seven main topics are familiar from Jack's past, as well as from America's future: cooperation in the workplace, healthcare, information workers/management, quality, reward systems, technology and training. In all, says the report, 177,335 lines of communication inform these summaries and the seven sets of recommendations to the White House.

And even though the word "final report" is used as an official status, Jack stressed in his introductory remarks that "it is definitely not final in another sense. It is merely one stage in a process that began four months ago and will have no ending until some of these recommendations are improved, implemented or abandoned. As one participant said at the end, 'I am damn well not going to have spent all this time just spitting in the wind. I intend, for one at least, to DO something... Anybody else game?'"

Considering the advances APC made later in the concept and development of knowledge management (KM) and the fact that Jack and Carla ended up writing a respected book on the subject, it's fascinating to note that many senior executives felt their companies "knew" a good deal more than they officially or scientifically knew.

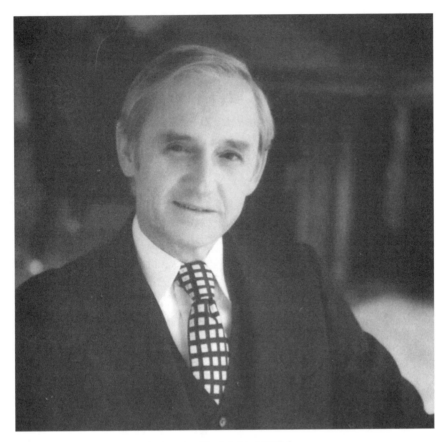

A portrait of Jack in his APQC days

That is, employees at all levels had worked out solutions to specific problems, many minor but some major, and applied those solutions day after day to get the job done. Because of failings in sharing such knowledge and putting it into official practices, many concepts and techniques pioneered in the United States (i.e. participative management, quality, robotics and transistor technology) had found their warmest welcome in Japan, in some cases their only warm welcome. The vision was stark: "If Americans fail to implement, then we will continue to fall short, no matter how many funds we invest in research, education, employee programs, quality, etc." As one participant expressed it: "What we lack is not basic knowledge, but the

determination, persistence and ingenuity to use productively what we already know."

Jack, of course, hated academic or scholarly pursuits that never dug deeper than platitudes as well as those that called for action when it was clear no action was likely. He and Carla pushed their teams to talk about things that were painful, that were almost certain to make people angry. One of these topics was labor management relations and the entire idea of "employment security." Business leaders knew that, day to day, what employment security there was in the American economy was the province of labor unions—and labor unions, after all, were to many the enemy.

The leaders were reluctant to give unions a larger place at the table, seeing such a move as causing "higher fixed costs, reduced flexibility, freezing in inefficient workers, an erosion of management prerogatives and an invitation to employee complacency." Voices were raised in this group, yet when the group studied the issue more deeply, it discovered that things were not as black-and-white as they seemed. Some companies with unions and high employment security did indeed have high productivity, while others fell depressingly short. Workers don't, in other words, have to be running scared to do a good job. Some other factor was making them more productive than they "had to be" to hold onto their jobs. Jack believed it was a sense of empowerment and respect, the same motivation that had driven the Price Commission and daily drove workers in Japan.

In yet another preview of APC projects to come, the group added a topic to its final report recommending creation of a "National Medal for Quality Achievement," to be presented to one or more American business leaders each year for their company's improvement in productivity. The medal champions began with what, at the same time, was most disturbing and most obvious. "Many members of society are unaware of the important role productivity plays in their economic well-being and the economic well-being of the United States," they wrote. "A preliminary step to improving productivity demands greater awareness of this issue among all sectors of the nation."

Jack recognized a project. One of his first concrete steps after presenting his group's report to the Reagan White House was pushing to create such a national award and raising the money to administer it. First, however, came the presentation, scheduled to be held in one of the numberless office blocks in Washington near the State Department. Jack and Carla would speak about their high-tech methodology (thanking GE and Apple) and their panel's findings. Reagan would show up and officially accept the report but, as is common with presidential schedules, no one could be sure exactly when. Jack arranged with the Secret Service to let him know when Reagan was on his way. Instead, the only word he got was when the President of the United States was walking into the meeting room. Carla was in the middle of her presentation, but she stopped the moment she saw the President. He accepted the group's enthusiastic applause, moved to the podium, delivered a few general remarks thanking all those who participated and left. Carla inched back up to the microphone. "Now," she said, "before I was so rudely interrupted..." The line got the biggest laugh of the day.

Creating the national award had a precedent, in the very place giving this country its greatest competition. The Deming Prize in Japan, presented by the Emperor himself, did exactly what Jack and his panel felt an American medal should and would do: spur competition among companies in the realm of productivity and quality. Jack went it alone for almost two years, having also been told by the White House not to come back about this until he had the detailed plan and all the money to implement it in place.

Like those mirages that move on forever ahead of us on a sunny highway, the White House brought on another delay once Jack had accomplished those things. Yes, they said, make an award. But the President of the United States can't present it without the full authorization of Congress. Initially frustrated by what seemed one-hoop-too-many to jump through, Jack remembered his lessons from Politics 101 and his days at the helm of price controls. He and other quality-minded people got the okay for the bill creating an American

National Quality Award introduced and passed through the House of Representatives. In the Senate it was sent to the Commerce Committee, where one noteworthy change was made. Former Commerce Secretary Malcolm Baldrige had recently died in a rodeo accident, so a move was made to name the award in honor of him. Jack had known the man only casually but was fine with the change. The Malcolm Baldrige National Quality Award became a reality, with full congressional approval. The award was set up and is administered by the National Institute of Standards and Technology (NIST), an agency of the U.S. Department of Commerce. In 1988, the first three recipients of the prestigious award were Motorola, the commercial nuclear fuel division of Westinghouse and, in the small business category, a company called Globe Metallurgical. (From 1988 through 2013 a total of ninety-five Baldrige Award winners have been named, close to 1000 organizations have applied and thousands more have relied of the criteria to improve.) In recognition of how far the "quality movement" had come in a short, dramatic time, APC officially became the American Productivity & Quality Center (APQC) in 1988.

To help spur Baldrige program participation early on, APQC helped organize the first Quest for Excellence conference in 1989 where the original winners gave insights on how they won the award to an audience of some 1000 attendees in DC. For the first three years of the award's existence, APQC and the American Society for Quality Control (ASQ) worked together managing aspects of the program for NIST, and after that, ASQ continued the program on its own. By that time, Jack had decided states needed to honor their best businesses as well, starting with an award in Texas. In time, the list of states issuing annual quality honors reached as high as forty-two, many asking APQC to help them with criteria and training of quality examiners.

According to the NIST website, the impact of the Baldrige program, criteria and award has been far reaching: In *Building on Baldrige: American Quality for the 21st Century*, the private Council on Competitiveness said, "More than any other program, the Baldrige

Award is responsible for making quality a national priority and disseminating best practices across the United States." An October 2001 study of the economic impact of the Baldrige Program, prepared for NIST by Albert N. Link and John T. Scott, conservatively estimated the net private benefits associated with the program to the economy as a whole at $24.65 billion. When compared to the social costs of the program of $119 million, the Baldrige Program's social benefit-to-cost ratio is 207-to-1. A later study of the Baldrige Program's value to US organizations by Link and Scott released in December 2011 found an even greater benefit-to-cost ratio of 820 to 1 based on the inclusion and growth of health care, education, and non-profit participation in Baldrige.

Back in 1974, at the end of his book *Confessions of a Price Controller*, Jack devoted thirty-seven pages of fine print and graphs to explaining the problems American business faced and why price controls would never be the solution. In the fourteen years of work before he and Carla would write their best-selling *American Business: A Two-Minute Warning*, his detailed summary had been distilled into a mere three bullet points:

1. US productivity growth was then on a declining trend, but most Americans were not aware of it.
2. Foreign competitors were outperforming the United States in productivity and quality. Most Americans were unaware or unconcerned.
3. Government controls, subsidies and protection were not the answer. Officials were not convinced.

Published in 1988 by The Free Press, a division of Macmillan, *American Business: A Two-Minute Warning* delivers all the urgency that its title promises. The United States, Jack and Carla argue, is a football team that has led comfortably for the entire game, only to find itself with a mere one-point lead in the final two minutes. What the nation chooses and manages to do now, not in any of the minutes

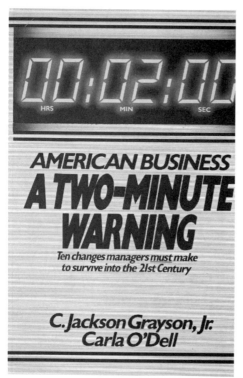

American Business: A Two-Minute Warning (1988)

that went before, will decide whether it wins the game. W or L. That's all. The rest is just statistics. Jack and Carla let their mission shape even their dedication of the book: "We dedicate our thoughts and hopes to the future—to the men and women working across America whose actions will ultimately determine the outcome of the last two minutes of the game."

The book is serious stuff, despite the readable style and occasional reminders that Jack and Carla are optimists rather than pessimists about America. There's no shortage of terms borrowed from economics and explained in lay terms, with the stated goal of informing and influencing business people and union leaders, not only academics. And since Jack is one of the authors, no reader should be surprised that *American Business: A Two-Minute Warning* is sometimes very funny. Today, Jack is particularly proud of his contribution concerning the history of global financial power, titled "The Decline and Fall of Practically Everybody." Since Jack understood that Greece and Rome were eternal whipping boys of those with a moral rather than financial agenda, he concentrates most of his analysis of the past on Great Britain, which led the world in productivity, created an empire upon which "the sun never set" and then had to watch its sun drop beneath the horizon anyway. Fascinatingly, England's most serious competitor by the end—its "Japan," so to speak—was the colony it had dismissed so often as a non-starter, the United States.

Jack's treatment of Great Britain forms the heart of the title's warning, since he finds dozens of parallels to work with, from English economists whose published cautions were ignored at the time to politicians calling for protectionist policies instead of a free market, just as politicians were doing in America in the 1980s. Carla wrote a ten-point "Agenda for Adjustment" that was familiar around APQC by this point (peppered with quotes from sources ranging from Arnold Toynbee to Yogi Berra), summarizing their message. "The rate of productivity is highest when there is competition and lowest when there is none," they write. "Competition is the spur to growth and improvement. The drive of competitors can be contagious, and their practices are instructive. America will not be more productive through protection, retaliation or bashing foreign competitors. We can learn from them, correct our weaknesses and build on our strengths."

There had to be a way, Jack and Carla believed, for American business to learn from other companies, both here and abroad, whose experiences could make a difference. After all it was Japanese companies sharing their practices around productivity and quality that created more than just a notion in the American business leaders that Jack took to Japan, that productivity and quality were areas that were important and should become part of their line of sight. This concept of learning from others was now making its way into APQC's work, not to mention the Baldrige Award included criteria for "benchmarking." True benchmarking required the sharing of information from one company to another, an act that seemed to violate at least two top-line beliefs of corporate America. To tell your competitors of your best practices was to help them compete better—against you. Therefore, it should never be done. Jack comments with a laugh today: "We never expected companies to share their *patented* best practices."

Also, within specific industries there was the very tangible fear that talk about business among competitors would resemble "collusion" in a definition that might attract antitrust charges from the Justice Department. After applying its own antitrust attorneys and

those of several corporations to the subject, APQC was able to declare that as long as prices were not discussed, nothing in these conversations would constitute collusion. And it got the Justice Department to say so, even if unofficially. As usual, traveling from boardroom to boardroom, preaching the value of benchmarking required money so Jack, as always, set to the task of raising it. He gave a speech in one large room full of decision makers, stressing his findings about antitrust and challenging the leaders to come to the table with their checkbooks. The head of quality at Compaq, Greg Watson, pledged $5000 to the benchmarking effort, and by the end of the session most of the other companies followed suit. One company, horrified by the whole idea of talking with competitors, threatened to withdraw its support from APQC. Jack knew that the only road led forward from here. This laid the foundation of what became APQC's International Benchmarking Clearinghouse. Again, Jack's vision was grand. But, this time it had no borders and had global implications. The goal was to provide a resource for businesses, governments and nonprofits to share information for the purposes of improving and gaining in their quest for competitiveness—a place where they could go to learn about benchmarking, a place where they could share information safely.

What could it look like and how would companies actually use this benchmarking resource? To launch the effort in 1992 Jack and Carla brought together eighty-six companies to design the products and services of the International Benchmarking Clearinghouse. These same companies were offered the ability to join as "Founders." A sign of things to come, all eighty-six paid $5000 to join this exciting new part of APQC, the International Benchmarking Clearinghouse.

One of the first challenges APQC and the steering committee members embarked upon was getting their legal counsels to create guidelines for sharing of information. Jack was never one to run from a challenge, so he and Carla brought together the legal counsel of the companies in one room to design a code of conduct for benchmarking that they could endorse and that would give companies the ability to engage in this concept of benchmarking. Never mind the challenge of

getting eighty-six attorneys to agree to share their companies' prac-
tices; Jack and Carla forged ahead, and in the end they co-created
the APQC Benchmarking Code of Conduct to address the protocol
and legality of benchmarking. In a sense, APQC provided a neutral
ground, a Switzerland as it were, where companies could share prac-
tices without fear. Today the Code of Conduct is the framework for
sharing across tens of thousands of individuals and organizations who
engage in benchmarking as a tool for continuous improvement.

During one of those early member meetings Bob Ogle, a senior
vice president with Johnson & Johnson, suggested that APQC was
perfectly positioned to form cross-industry consortia of companies
and competitors all interested in learning best practices. This led to
the concept of site visits to see what companies were doing firsthand
and research targeted around specific interest areas; these consortia
studies have been a pillar of APQC research for understanding the
best practices inside organizations since that time. That point is not
lost on Jack who points out proudly that "Many of our best ideas at
APQC come from our members. It pays to listen."

To fund the new benchmarking effort, APQC had to get many
other companies to join in, not just the original supporters. It was
going to take professional salespeople, not just Jack. APQC was in
trouble financially, focused on doing research but without a business
model to sustain it for the long term.

At the beginning, APQC enjoyed a certain success in fundraising,
particularly with Jack's personal and business relationships with doz-
ens of important American corporations as legacy from his days in
Washington. In that period's aftermath, he had even been invited to
serve on many boards of directors—Lever Bros., Sun Oil Company,
Overhead Door, Oryx Energy, First City Bank, Infomart and BFI
among them as well as the Harris, Potlatch, Tyler and Whitman
Corporations—which provided some money for him and consider-
able access to top executives for contributions, as well as the oppor-
tunity to learn and have fun.

Jack recalls one such outing while he was on the board of Sun

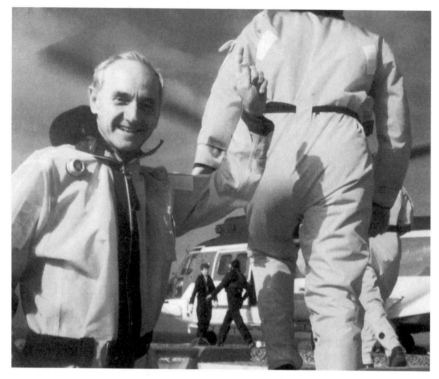

The North Sea

Oil. The company had purchased a considerable amount of oil in the North Sea and flew the board to Scotland to tour the operations, including an off-shore platform. As the board was suiting up in their orange jumpers, the safety head cautioned that, "You will only live about five minutes without the suit if you plunge into the frigid waters." Luckily, the group returned with no incident.

As a result of Jack's connections, APQC had (or seemed to have) enough money to operate indefinitely as a "mission-driven" organization. Early employees certainly felt that way, working as though they were on a mission to save the American economy. Few of these employees, whatever their intelligence, ever gave a moment's thought to how APQC might continue to fund its work.

As the 1980s turned into the 1990s, Jack and Carla were giving finances an increasing amount of thought. And worry. The

environment outside was changing just as fast as the environment inside of APQC, and donations and grants were harder to come by. Once again, Jack took radical action.

First, to allow Jack time to concentrate on his role as APQC visionary and builder, the APQC board of directors asked Carla to assume operational responsibility based on her track record running a successful consulting practice. Early responses to the crisis included cost-cutting and necessary layoffs. Still, she and Jack understood that cost-cutting is, at best, a temporary Band-Aid® and, at worst, the beginning of a downward spiral toward the end.

Next, Jack and Carla needed to find an energetic and experienced sales person to help APQC sell memberships to companies. They found Lisa Higgins who brought a background in both sales and process management. In less than two weeks, Lisa sized up the situation and told Jack and Carla that they needed to build a sales infrastructure inside APQC. A sales force had never existed in APQC's past and was foreign to those who had worked under the mission-driven culture of APQC. Lisa was convinced that now was the time to move to creating a model that would sustain APQC for years to come without donations and grants. Jack and Carla agreed, and Lisa forged ahead, almost immediately hiring ten salespeople and packaging information about the offerings they would be selling.

Lisa found herself on something of a secret mission—secret at the start anyway—that had everything to do with a life-and-death struggle to keep APQC afloat. Everything in both her financial and her sales backgrounds would be required to change the organization's own business model as drastically as that of any company they counseled. And she would need a really thick skin on top of that. It was risky; culturally APQC wasn't an organization that understood salespeople. Sales was a notion so foreign to its culture that the first ten salespeople Lisa brought on were greeted with more suspicion than smiles. "How could Jack Grayson the visionary allow common *salespeople* in the building?" complained mission-driven employees. At the start, Jack felt compelled to locate the sales staff on a separate

floor of the APQC building, only compounding the impression they were telemarketers laboring in a sweatshop. Some of the most avid believers in APQC's mission handed in their resignations, still seemingly unaware of the trouble the organization was in.

Over several years, despite feeling like a "three-headed monster," Jack, Carla and Lisa worked closely to revise APQC's operational model to become more fiscally sustainable. Individual memberships were among the first things to go, all 6000 to 8000 of them, replaced by corporate memberships. These memberships allowed all employees of that company access to APQC's research and processes. All new APQC services flowed from there, often based on identified needs in business, plus the demands of members to keep getting value for what they'd paid each year: consulting, training, seminars and the like. From that day forward, true to the pro-business stance Jack had maintained from his beginnings, the mantra became "To do good, you have to do well."

The people drawn to work at *this* APQC were those who understood and supported both doing well and good. Many people contributed hard work and considerable insights over the years, but few would become as melded to APQC's work and mission as the growing executive team. Within two years Lisa Higgins was named APQC's director of membership and part of the organization's executive team. Lisa was able to practice the productivity and quality gospel that Jack and Carla always preached. (Later she was named director of benchmarking services, chief operating officer in November 2000 and president in May 2012 with Carla being named CEO.) Joining the movement in the mid- to late-90s were Cathy Hill, Cindy Hubert, Mike Shea and Ron Webb. These additions proved crucial for Jack, in effect, to replicate himself, as all these men and women understood the next generation of APQC and the business model. And, all are still with APQC today—some fifteen to twenty years later—running concurrent pillars at APQC for benchmarking, knowledge management, membership and operations.

With a stroke of luck in 1993, *The Wall Street Journal* got wind

of the story about companies joining with APQC's International Benchmarking Clearinghouse and ran a front page article about APQC and the notion of benchmarking. The phones started ringing, and the benchmarking era of APQC was born. Now APQC had dozens of active member companies willing to help, with many more to follow.

Jack and his team conducted seminars on how to conduct benchmarking, completed individual benchmarking projects for companies and organized consortia best practice research studies. When an early consortia research project on knowledge management was launched in 1996, over forty companies signed up to sponsor the research at $15,000 each. This fast response proved that APQC had a hit on its hand in terms of both the subject matter and the research format. Plus, it proved a solution for APQC's ongoing financial needs as it grew to conduct approximately fifteen research projects annually across a range of hot topics.

Over time, benchmarking as understood early around APQC would make its way into many high places in businesses and in government. Within the federal government, the State Department and the Federal Reserve came around, as did others. The US Army saw the value of gathering and making accessible wisdom from soldiers in the foxholes. One particularly memorable benchmarking visit Carla and Jack made was to the National Security Agency (NSA), which still tended to deny existing at all. They were met at the airport in Washington and driven to somewhere Jack thinks was close to Baltimore in a closed black van. "I had a hell of a time selling them on this," he admits now. "But they finally came to see that benchmarking fits with them too." When he asked his NSA listeners exactly where he was, they said, "If we tell you, we'll have to kill you."

"It's an old joke around there, apparently," offers Jack.

Beyond government, military and businesses, Jack's ultimate vision was to use productivity and quality to improve ALL sectors of the economy, which meant the healthcare industry was on his radar next (followed later by education to complete his all sectors' goal). As

usual Jack attacked the effort with vigor and on a grand scale by hosting a powerhouse three-day conference in July 1994 titled "Creating a Healthcare System that Works." He secured forty-four advisory members to anchor the effort and raised $750,000 to produce the event. More than 1100 attendees convened at the George R. Brown Center in Houston to hear from Texas Governor Ann Richards and one hundred forty speakers across sixteen tracks and eighty workshops discuss how to use productivity and quality to improve healthcare operations, delivery and outcomes. The event included forty-eight sponsors and one hundred twenty exhibitors. With Jack's well-known proclivity to weave in fun along the way, Lisa Higgins kicked off the event dressed as a Southwest Airlines flight attendant with a humorous conference takeoff monologue.

Ultimately, APQC would teach the techniques and approaches of benchmarking and process management to tens of thousands of business people from no fewer than ninety-six countries. Understandably, there was a language barrier, both in sharing information with overseas companies and within the United States. For all combinations of reasons, companies felt within their rights to call things by any name they chose and measure things any way they wanted. Jack decided that a dictionary—or more academically, a "taxonomy"—was needed, so companies could share meaningful information about their processes and practices, internally as well as across industry and even international boundaries.

In 1992 Jack and Carla convened a group of members, business leaders and process management experts to create the Process Classification Framework®—or PCF—as a common language through which APQC members could benchmark their processes. Each brought their own enterprise maps at a high level with the goal to develop a common way to name and describe the major business processes to benchmark together. In fact, it served as a practical dictionary for measurement and discussion of best practices with executives as far away as Russia, China and India. Today the PCF is the most downloaded document APQC has ever produced, logging

more than 300,000 downloads from APQC's website since 2010 and tens of thousands of downloads—or hard copies in its pre-Internet days—earlier as well with more than a dozen industry-specific versions and several language translations. In some ways, it's an international language for business. Or, in Jack's words: "It's the Esperanto of Processes."

As APQC was conducting its consortia benchmarking projects and site visits over these years, Jack, Carla and Lisa came to see the next natural phase for APQC: standard quantitative benchmarking. Each of the best practice site visits that APQC conducted included a detailed questionnaire for all participants on the subject matter of that study. Many of the questions asked for quantitative data, which provided more tangible insights for a company but proved hard to compare in terms of the metrics used and also the sample size. So, Carla and Lisa set out to design a more rigorous, global approach to developing metrics and collecting data.

As it did at the founding of APQC, IBM (under the leadership of Ginni Rometty, then vice president of consulting services and later CEO) once again played a pivotal role in taking the notion of benchmarking to the next level in 2004, underwriting the launch of APQC's Open Standards Benchmarking®. Just as it did a decade earlier, the announcement of the new benchmarking effort made its way to the front page of *The Wall Street Journal* on May 19, 2004. "In an effort to boost productivity IBM and fourteen other corporations, government organizations and consultants have agreed to form a collaborative to share and standardize performance benchmarks, in the same way that open-source software programmers share code," led the story that appeared on the front page of *WSJ* Europe. Joining the effort were powerhouse companies Bank of America, Boehringer-Ingelheim, Booz Allen Hamilton, CEMEX, Fuji Xerox Co., Gartner, KPMG, M.D. Anderson Medical Center, P&G Worldwide, Raytheon Company, SAP, Shell Oil Co, the US Navy and the World Bank.

The goal for this new effort was to further Jack's original vision for improving productivity and quality around the world, this

time by taking benchmarking to the next level through a standardized approach to capture quantitative measures and the data to support performance against them. The Open Standards vision was to allow companies to use a standard set of measures for standard sets of processes—based upon APQC's widely-adopted PCF—that existed in all companies regardless of geography or industry, to access benchmarks for performance. Productivity measures were included for each of the processes. Jack also wanted to ensure the benchmarking was accessible across functional areas so the database spans from financial management, human capital management and information technology to supply chain management, product development and sales and marketing. Today, the Open Standards is the world's largest database of benchmarks anywhere in the world with more than 17,000 participants and over 1500 standardized measures spanning people, process and technology.

APQC's successful experiences with benchmarking in the early 90s raised a troubling question: sometimes companies actually had best practices in one division but other divisions or plants didn't even know they existed, much less how to access and adopt them. Even more troubling, when they did know about it, the practices did not necessarily transfer. The quest to understand *why* once again put Jack and Carla on the road, this time to visit companies, such as Buckman Laboratories and McKinsey and Company, who had been successful sharing what they know and who were mentioned by management guru Tom Peters in his book *Thriving on Chaos*. The journey to understand knowledge management and the processes to help knowledge flow became Jack and Carla's next quest.

Like most subjects and most issues Jack and Carla decided to tackle, knowledge management was not a completely new concept, nor was it likely to be entirely figured out anytime soon. It was an ongoing challenge for American business, affecting entire corporations, the departments within their structure and, of course, the individual employees who make so many decisions minute-to-minute and day-to-day.

More and more, pursuing greater productivity at both the blue-

collar and white-collar level, Jack was running into problems with what he came to call knowledge. Sometimes, he understood, there wasn't any—or there simply wasn't enough of it. Other times, he could clearly see knowledge spread throughout an organization chart, literally from the ground up, yet it never came together: the left hand didn't know what the right hand was doing or learning. Sometimes, people did not even know there *were* better practices inside their own organization, much less know what management methods could help those best practices transfer across all the sites that could use them. Yet, Jack and Carla knew there were some pioneering corporate examples of best practice transfer and knowledge sharing. The foundational ideas behind knowledge management (KM), which Jack and Carla would turn into the book *If Only We Knew What We Know* in 1998, were in place.

Promoting the importance of KM throughout the early 1990s, Jack and Carla saw clearly that this was an idea whose time had come and was ready for a larger platform. Jack had the brilliant idea of convening a symposium on knowledge management at APQC to once again bring companies and thought leaders together to share their experiences with KM and identify emerging methods that worked. Once again engaged in a pioneering venture, Jack needed to enlist the help of others. Robert Hiebeler, then a partner with Arthur Andersen, saw the need and power of such a symposium. Convinced that such a forum was just what was needed to raise awareness and start a movement, Hiebeler agreed to underwrite any losses if there were any. Fortunately, there were none. Over 500 people paid and attended the symposium held at The Houstonian Hotel in 1995, and the global knowledge management movement was born, with APQC in the forefront.

In a sense, KM defined and described a lot of APQC's projects throughout the 1990s and 2000s as led by Carla and Cindy Hubert, from its commitment to benchmarking to over forty funded research projects on KM to its eventual online library (the Knowledge Base). Such efforts have made APQC a consistent winner in the annual international MAKE (Most Admired Knowledge Enterprises)

awards given by the Teleos Research Organization in England and *KM World*'s list of 100 Companies That Matter in Knowledge Management. In 2000, Teleos also granted a one-time MAKE award to the 10 Most Admired Knowledge Individuals in the world, listing among the winners people like Jack Welch of GE, Yotaro Kobayashi of Fuji Xerox, John Chambers of Cisco and Jack Grayson of APQC.

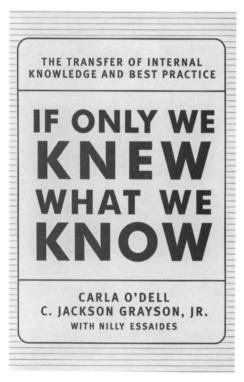

THE TRANSFER OF INTERNAL
KNOWLEDGE AND BEST PRACTICE

IF ONLY WE
KNEW
WHAT WE
KNOW

CARLA O'DELL
C. JACKSON GRAYSON, JR.
WITH NILLY ESSAIDES

If Only We Knew What We Know (1998)

In the year it took Jack and Carla to research and write *If Only We Knew What We Know* in 1998 (again for The Free Press, now a subsidiary of Simon & Schuster), they surveyed, interviewed and visited hundreds of organizations, compiling numbers and anecdotes of success or failure concerning knowledge management and the transfer of best practices. These anecdotes with observations form what are probably the most enjoyable parts of the book. Besides defining knowledge and KM and outlining real stories of "the transfer of internal knowledge and best practices," *If Only* talks about barriers to that transfer. In collaboration with Gabriel Szulanski, now a Wharton professor, Jack and Carla identify four main barriers: ignorance that such information might be useful to others; the absence of money, time and management resources to absorb such knowledge; the lack of preexisting relationships among workers that make the conversation easier; and the general lack of motivation when companies or individuals see no clear business reason for transferring knowledge and best practices.

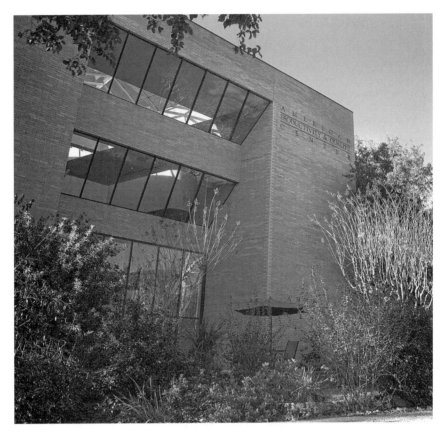

APQC Building in 2014

Even more specifically, Jack and Carla zero in on four enablers necessary for the transfer of company knowledge—infrastructure, culture, technology and measurement. Tellingly, for the late 1990s as for today, they focus most on culture. Hidden away within each company's self-identity are keys to how well (or poorly) it will embrace knowledge management.

"Culture is the combination of shared history, expectation, unwritten rules and social mores that affects the behavior of everyone, from managers to mailroom clerks," they write.

"It's the set of underlying beliefs that, while never exactly articulated, are always there to color the perception of actions

and communications... If your organization's natural tendency is to share and collaborate, all you have to do is eliminate structural barriers and provide enablers (like technology and facilitators) to allow practices and ideas to flow seamlessly across time and space. But if your company's nature is to hoard knowledge, then the best and greatest KM application may not be enough to alter your employees' behavior."

In pursuit of their research, Jack often confronted what seemed elemental roadblocks to the gathering and sharing of knowledge, many going back to a worker's first day on the job. Some barriers to learning, however, seemed to go back much farther than that, to long before that employee was old enough to work. And that education or lack thereof, Jack would decide, was a huge part of the problem.

16

FUTURE SCHOOL

WITH A STABLE MANAGEMENT TEAM AND business model in place at APQC, Jack was free to pursue his desire to improve the US education system. And his marriage to Carla both provided stability and gave him a wife as committed to his missions as he was. This mutual dedication proved the best way to let both of them work without fearing they were taking time away from their marriage. Going to the office, meeting with high-level business people, traveling to foreign countries to study their industries and, ultimately, educational systems, and then

Antarctica: Jack and Carla on the bow

Left to right: Jack, Michael, Randy

Left to right: Daniel, Randy, Michael

talking and writing about what they see, contributes to rather than detracts from Jack and Carla's marriage. They still make ample time to travel and play outside of business as well. By 2003, Jack and Carla completed their goal to explore the world and all its seven continents with an adventure trip to Antarctica.

Even though his schedule was always full over the years, Jack made it a priority to bring the boys to the farm regularly. He wanted

them to experience a taste of the country life and upbringing so dear and core to Jack. Over time, Jack's heartfelt commitment to Fort Necessity came to require less of his attention. He had always considered the farm his old home place, not only where his ancestors had lived and worked but also where his parents continued to live, his mother resigned to never moving to a city the way she had wished and his father still master of all he could survey. In 1983, all of that had changed.

Jack's parents

On Halloween that year, a fast-spreading fire destroyed the original family home built by Wiley Blount Grayson in 1836, leaving little but charred chimneys and bits of antique furniture. The home, listed on the National Register of Historic Places, was unoccupied at the time of the fire but was in the process of being remodeled by the relative who now owned it. "Because of the cypress wood used in the home, the fire burned rapidly," an official with the Winnsboro Fire Department told *The Franklin Sun* newspaper. "There was little we could do." Though Jack's parents had lived for decades in their own, less historic home across the highway, Jack and the rest of the family had always looked upon the Grayson House as a reminder that life goes on. That reminder was now missing from the farm's landscape.

A year later Jack's mother's health began to fail. She had already traveled down to New Orleans and been diagnosed with atherosclerosis of the brain, a condition that limited blood flow and therefore the oxygen needed to keep functioning. She lived in the shadow of death, eventually not even recognizing her husband. "Who is that man?" she'd ask Jack during his visits, gesturing to his father. "He'd better get out of here because Charlie's going to be home soon." The condition

led to her death in the fall of 1984, and her family buried her in the Grayson Cemetery on the land she had lived on her entire married life.

Jack's father had continued living on the farm and refusing to give up running it. Charlie Grayson enjoyed remarkably good health outside

Jack with his parents

of his worsening heart problems. His doctors cautioned him about the need to lose weight, and he certainly did what he could. But with a fading grasp of the farm's day-to-day operation and no wife to make him take care of himself, it proved a losing battle. One day he was out surveying the farm by car and turned across the path of an oncoming car. Charlie's car flipped into a ditch from the impact, requiring an ambulance from Winnsboro to rescue him and rush him to the hospital in critical condition. Jack, when he arrived in Winnsboro after hearing of the accident, was faced with a painful decision. His father was on life support and, according to his doctors, would probably never be more than a vegetable. "They said he would never be able to live a normal life," Jack recalled. "And I knew he would not want to live that way." On April 15, 1985, he decided to let the doctors remove the life support.

Charlie Grayson was laid to rest next to his wife in the Grayson Cemetery, a fenced piece of land in the middle of a cotton field that he and his sharecropping families had spent their lives tending. Simple headstones, like those of all the Graysons buried there, mark their graves.

The deaths of his parents would not be Jack's final encounter with losing a loved one. Some years later, once APQC was up and running successfully, his son Daniel came to work there. Incredibly

bright and creative, well versed in all things computer, Daniel brought an amazing skill set to work for the center. He did, however, suffer from severe asthma, forcing him to go through each day with an inhaler ever at hand and later other aids to his breathing. This terrible condition, doctors told Jack in retrospect, inspired Daniel to seek escape into drugs. Eventually, the drug problems outweighed all others, and Jack felt compelled to fire his own son and send him into rehab. This seemed to help. Daniel went to Dallas to live with his mother Cynthia, who had remarried since her divorce from Jack and given birth to another son, Nicholas. Tragically, Daniel's half-brother found him dead in his room, suffocated from asthma.

In addition to the pain of his personal loss, Jack mourns Daniel's undeveloped potential. "What a wasted life for a bright guy," Jack says. "We lost a person with a lot of potential. Everybody wanted to work with him because he was so smart."

Along with the losses of his later life, Jack has also experienced the joy of becoming a grandfather four times. Mckenna Nicole arrived in 2001 to Kelly and Chris Grayson; Andrew Jackson, in 2011 to Siew Leng Toh and Michael Grayson; and Clove Regan and Annika Regan, in 2013 to Kerry O'Regan and Randall Grayson.

If anything, this intimacy with the circle of life has caused Jack to throw himself into his latest mission with more energy than ever. In its most basic form, the APQC education initiative emerged early as part of other things. The ongoing study of American competitiveness, for example, forced Jack and APQC to focus on this country's greatest competitors in the 1970s and 1980s, Japan along with China, Korea, Singapore, India and Germany. And while those countries' business practices impressed Jack—success has always impressed him—they also pointed to the workforce that made productivity, quality and success even possible. Nothing, Jack decided, had more to do with Japan's emergence as a global economic power from the rubble of World War II than its emphasis on and approach to education.

"The Japanese," he and Carla write in *American Business: A Two-Minute Warning*:

"have the most complete, effective and demanding system of elementary and secondary education in the world. Nor is learning confined to schools. The Japanese emphasize learning from birth to death—at home, in school, at work and in their daily lives. There is a national consensus on the importance of learning."

For those who might question his judgment, then or now, Jack outlined the superiority of the Japanese system in four of five major categories: parents and the home, elementary and secondary, education in business and education in daily life. Only in higher education did the United States maintain an edge by the late 1980s, Jack determined, which explained the "heavy traffic" of foreign students earning bachelors and graduate degrees here. He was clearly expecting the response he often got to his warnings, that American tendency to find something to brag about and to ignore everything else. What we didn't know, Jack cautioned, might indeed kill us—at least as a power in a world economy we had virtually controlled since the end of the war. The very juggernaut of 1950s growth, Jack argued, had obscured the first signs of danger.

The United States, even as it prospered in its quality of life, was starting to fall behind in science and engineering—a fact that not even our fascination with NASA and the space program could entirely cover up. SAT scores were trending downward, and (perhaps even more disturbing) what came to be known as "functional illiteracy" was trending upward. From there, once Jack had caught the drift, all the signs became warning signs. In addition to superficial knowledge of nearly all important subject areas, he found in his research low teacher pay, inadequate teacher skills, high dropout rates, only a focus on outcomes and not processes, poor reading and writing—and, once young people had joined the workforce, low investment in training compared to competitor nations. As he had so often, he found just the right quote in assessing the fading British Empire, which had provided "education for industrial decline."

Jack looked closely at such competitors and then back at the workers he encountered in his own country. "What was the difference?" he asked. What were we failing to give kids in school that they would need to live happy and productive lives? He identified seven things a competitive nation needed its people to have: a high degree of average functional literacy; some basic competency with mathematics, statistics and the scientific method; the ability to observe and implement processes, analyze, interpret and take action; a knowledge of the world; the ability to work together in teams; empowerment of all people; the ability to accept responsibility; and the ability to learn constantly and adjust to change. Thinking of the Japanese workforce and quoting one scholar, Jack argued that a "society where everyone reads and writes will beat a society where most are illiterates and a few are geniuses."

Years before it became the APQC Education Initiative in 2009, Jack was pressing for dramatic changes in the US system and the forces that resisted change. As he'd discovered all too well as business dean at SMU, a lot of people were satisfied with their comfortable berth even when the ship was undeniably sinking.

Among his many early recommendations were: lengthen the school year, the school week and the school day (competition required nothing less); increase homework; increase class size (bucking what "most people believe incorrectly" about smaller classes equaling better education); increase the "socialization" engendered by project learning, experimental learning, cooperation and group-based learning; and learn to organize by processes, not functional silos.

With his experience in Washington ever before his eyes, Jack was quick to remind anyone who would listen that the primary control of the educational system rested with the students and the faculty and the state and local governments, not at the federal level. He saw the federal government as the natural home for student aid, long-term programs to combat illiteracy and large-scale training for workers dislocated by industrial change. Leaders at the state and local level, on the other hand, would be in charge of setting curriculum

requirements and statewide standards, strengthening teacher competency, funding and supporting greater productivity in education ("better-educated students for less funds") and raising teachers' salaries to "about the average of business middle managers in the state." All of these areas, as Jack no doubt foresaw, would prove difficult and at times controversial. But he did not see any way for America to avoid facing the painful truth.

"The United States must recall that it once gave higher priority to education and that the 'wealth of nations' is truly their human assets," Jack wrote in 1988. "Just as business must adjust its methods and style to fit a new world, so must education. Of all the challenges facing the United States competitively, improving education ranks at the top."

By the late 1990s and new millennium, the greatest change to American education's competitive position was that it wasn't just about the Japanese anymore. Other Asian nations, like Singapore, had systems that produced better-educated and better-motivated young people, especially when it came time for them to enter the workforce. Many European countries, led by Finland and others in Scandinavia, also became powers for America to reckon with, particularly with the strengthening evolution of the old Common Market into the European Union. If anything, the "two-minute warning" Jack and Carla had given to American business in 1988 was becoming the "one-minute warning." Something had to be done, and surveying the playing field, Jack decided he might be the man to do it.

Early on in his education thinking, Jack concentrated understandably on the world he knew best and most frustratingly, universities and graduate business schools. He had tried to install his revolutionary approaches as far back in his career as Tulane and, with considerable controversy, at SMU.

The education research first started in 1996 as an APQC consortia study for higher education on best practices for admitting and registering students. The group conducted site visits to hotels registering guests and hospitals admitting patients in hopes of learning how

other industries tackle a similar process. Jack recalls it being a huge breakthrough for universities to see that they could learn from other industries. Over the next decade, APQC would continue to conduct consortia benchmarking projects. What he came to realize, however, was that in many ways fixing education at the university level would be much too late. In fact, he wondered if that had been his problem all along. For professors, administrators, governments and students, college was the dysfunction it was because of everything that had gone before. APQC, Jack realized, had to start addressing the education problem earlier, by kindergarten at least and even, if possible, before that.

Traveling for research, conducting studies and offering solid alternatives to the existing system required money, and APQC simply didn't have it to spend. Jack had always been a master fundraiser, whether it was for business schools or his own organization, but this time he started out differently. With his parents and the old Grayson homestead gone from Fort Necessity, and with them so much of his attachment to the place, Jack determined to sell multi-acre plots to fund the education initiative. By the time APQC was ready to release its groundbreaking, all-encompassing report titled *Transforming Education* in 2013, Jack had turned every acre he owned in Fort Necessity into cash for the cause.

An early effort was called North Star and attracted considerable attention and no small amount of respect. Under the banner of PPM, the kind of "process and performance management" that was already changing business, healthcare, government and the military, APQC researched and selected ten school districts large and small, spread across the nation. Over four months in 2009, these districts received PPM coaching on three projects of their own choosing. By all accounts, the results were extraordinary.

"I have been in education for forty-two years," commented Michael Perich of the Montgomery County Public Schools in Maryland, "but I have never seen a project like APQC's North Star that has the potential to completely transform the education system

in this country." Kirby Lehman, former superintendent of the Jenks Public Schools in Oklahoma, understood North Star's mission and promise as well: "Some of the fundamental threats to the very core of our democratic republic relate to the continuing challenges we all face with public education and the direct relationship between public education and the nation's economy." Putting it even more succinctly, Terry Holliday, commissioner of education for the state of Kentucky, said the North Star project "can deliver on education reform where many other initiatives have failed."

North Star drew on many of the resources Jack had developed in and around his years dealing with corporate America and the many think tanks arrayed around it. He made several trips to MIT to discuss his ideas with process guru Michael Hammer, author of such business bestsellers as *Reengineering the Corporation* and *Beyond Reengineering*. After meeting with Jack in Cambridge, Hammer offered early interest and support. West Coast business consultant Peter S. Pande and his staff, who had improved the operations of GE, Cisco, adidas, Starwood Hotels, Charles Schwab, Marks & Spencer, BP and many others and penned several bestsellers based on his process management concept, also joined the North Star effort.

Within a few years, APQC's Education Initiative had successfully trained 109 school districts of all sizes across the United States as well as fifty schools in Australia. As productivity and quality have remained a fascination of Jack's, never more than in tight-money times, he says those districts flying the North Star flag in the US saved a documented $136 million on instruction and operations, for an average savings of $1.4 million per district and returned some 40,000 hours back to the classroom by just embarking on a few pilot projects each. The goal, as APQC expanded toward the *Transforming Education* model was to not only train more districts in America and around the world but to expand its ongoing reform to no fewer than thirty-two entities with a stake in the process. The report and initiative sets out the business case, backs it up with scores of successful projects in school districts and makes the fundraising ask for the $15.5 million. In essence this is

Jack's last, most ambitious and most impactful effort to truly improve the United States for future generations.

In the 2013 report's executive summary, Jack and his compatriots at APQC outline the issues with respect to their severity and magnitude. "Education is critically important for the preservation of our standard of living and our global competitiveness," he writes.

> "The current education system is in serious decline. If nothing changes, the United States will lose its global leadership in education and eventually its standard of living and its global competitiveness. If we are to turn the system around, it will have to be transformed as a system. Piecemeal or one-off disconnected reforms won't reverse the decline."

If anything, *Transforming Education* goes to its greatest length to establish and explain the connections that many had missed up until this point. It identifies no fewer than ten different "education providers" that need to get in on the ground floor of significant change: PreK-12, public and private universities, community colleges, colleges of education, charter schools, private schools, faith-based schools, military schools, libraries and career/tech training institutions. This possibly familiar list, however, is augmented by no fewer than twenty-two "stakeholders and governing agencies." A lifetime of struggling with the politics behind education had taught Jack that nothing was likely to get done or get better without "buy-in" from the twenty-two entities he had battled so fervently in his previous lives, including accrediting agencies, legislators, business groups, policy organizations, school boards, governors and labor unions.

None of these groups and the individuals within them could be reform's enemies, he understood. They had to be reform's partners, along with congressmen, governors, mayors, state and federal departments of education and even the students and their parents. Discord would not save American education. Nor would the electioneering that has become more and more common. And nor would the turf

wars that inspire resistance for resistance's sake and, at education's worst, the complete impossibility of any significant action.

Certainly nothing seemed old, familiar or stale in APQC's approach to education; if anything, many things would seem impossible except for the fact that Jack doesn't recognize that as a real word. All the same, the education plan does operate on ten proven methodologies utterly essential to the day-to-day operation of modern business, even if few educators and their handlers know anything about them. Readers of Jack and Carla's books over the years would be comfortable with them, though: benchmarking, knowledge management, an education process and outcomes database, process analytics, leadership academy, supply chain, empowerment, union-management collaboration, Ask Why 5 Times (a Japanese technique that keeps seeking truth about why something is or is not done), and an education-specific Process Classification Framework—a taxonomy that gives all involved in education a common vocabulary so they can share experiences and knowledge.

"It's a culture of can versus a culture of can't," Jack offers, touching his hand gently to *Transforming Education* as though it's his life's work, which in so many ways it is. "Education doesn't work as a system today, and until it does, these politicians can keep doing what they're doing. People need to realize they have the freedom to complain and criticize, the freedom to propose, the freedom to think on their own. Now *that* truly is empowerment. You can ask why about anything," Jack's eyes gleam, what they've always done best. "And then you can start to change it. It's freedom at work."

17

INTO THE AIR

O N OCTOBER 8, 2013, SOME EIGHTY FAMILY members, colleagues and friends gathered in the town of Sealy, west of Houston, to celebrate Jack Grayson's ninetieth birthday. In a sense, though, only Jack dared attend his own birthday party.

Whether he was thinking metaphorically or simply wished to fulfill a long-held dream, Jack's birthday celebration was jumping out of what he assured reporters and cameramen was a "perfectly good airplane." At ninety, it was not clear whether he was close to being the oldest person to ever skydive, nor did such things seem to matter much on that clear, sunny day. What mattered to Jack was the message: that anybody can do anything in America, as long as you want to do it enough, as long as you work hard enough to make it happen.

With nearly all of the APQC staff and close friends safely standing on the ground, Jack felt himself lifted to 14,000 feet above a patchwork of Texas fields and farms, watching the Gloster Aerodrome grow smaller with every foot of the ascent. Then, finally, with one member of the Westside Skydivers strapped to his back and several others hovering alongside (one running a video camera), Jack left the confines of the plane and began a dive that reached 120 mph before the parachute popped open to yank the men upward.

Spotlighted during TV reports on most Houston stations, as well as around Texas, the video shows Jack's skin and remaining strands

Jack and Carla before the jump

of hair pulled back tight by the force of the wind. Unlike the NASA astronauts, who first taught Americans what "Gs" look like in action, however, Jack was not straining or struggling. He was smiling the entire way down. The skydive ended in a graceful glide as the green grass grew closer and the patchwork became a single welcoming field. And then there was Jack, his colorful parachutes fluttering down around him like so many flags from battles fought long ago.

As he'd done so often throughout the decades, Jack used this moment to teach, to preach and to promote, dubbing his birthday event the *"Freedom to Dream, Courage to Act"* Flight, as he prepared these memoirs. He talked to reporters about his expectation to live to be 113—older than *that* if science could come up with "spare parts" from 3D printers. Jack invited his doctor who shares that dream, Dr. Bradley Bale, to celebrate the skydive day with him. All of the news reports spoke, at least briefly, about Jack still going into the office at APQC each day. Jack and APQC were still making news, after all these years.

"Your attitude is one of the greatest things that will keep you alive," Jack told one reporter moments after his skydive, sharing the practical wisdom of his nine decades. "Never think of the end. Always think of what you're doing."

Jack's 90th Birthday Skydive: October 8, 2013

The founder of APQC has embraced the freedom to dream and the courage to act, the right to ponder unorthodox issues in even more unorthodox ways, to tackle problems so big that few individuals caught in their web would dare wiggle, much less fight. And he has lived a life true to his understanding of what life should be, from his earliest efforts to write fiction, to his time as a naval officer, a newspaper reporter, an FBI agent, an import-export agent, a racehorse owner, a private pilot and a respected academic. He has dated Broadway actresses who must have filled some part of his hunger for all things theatrical, taken skilled teachers in the arts of love, married wives, had children and, finally, found a strong, loving partner. Without knowing where he was going, but with a strong sense of what mattered to him, Jack left the farm in the dust filling his rearview mirror and engaged fully in a vast array of worldly experiences. From the White House to corporate board rooms to podiums facing hundreds, even thousands, gathered excitedly to hear him speak, Jack remains that country boy who learned of his ancestor's adventures and took them to heart.

In conversation, Jack Grayson might be tempted to tell you that his life, and especially his resume, make no sense. Yet, the smile he invariably wears suggests that he hopes that when you reach your ninetieth birthday, your life story and your resume will be just like his: a clear reflection of both what you have dreamed and the courage to act and to achieve what those dreams have inspired.

AT-A-GLANCE TIMELINE
MILESTONES
FOR C. JACKSON GRAYSON'S
CAREER AND APQC

1923	Born on October 8 in Fort Necessity, Louisiana
1939	Attended Georgia Military Academy
1940-1943	Graduated from Tulane University with a bachelor's degree
1943-1946	Served in the U.S. Navy in the South Pacific during World War II
1947	Graduated from the Wharton School of Business at the University of Pennsylvania with a master's degree
1947-1949	Earned CPA certification and taught accounting at Tulane University
1949-1950	Became a newspaper reporter with *The New Orleans Item*
1950-1952	Served the Federal Bureau of Investigation (FBI) as a special agent
1952	Returned to Fort Necessity to manage the C.J. Grayson Farm
1953-1957	Returned to the faculty of Tulane. Earned a pilot's license and owned racehorses, including Nirboy
1958-1959	Joined Harvard University as assistant professor and doctoral student with the School of Business Administration
1960	Graduated from Harvard Business School with a doctorate
1960	Published first book, *Decisions Under Uncertainty: Drilling Decisions by Oil and Gas Operators,* by Harvard Business School

1961-1963	Returned to Tulane University as associate dean of the School of Business Administration
1963-1964	Named professor of IMEDE's Management Development Institute in Switzerland via Harvard
1964-1968	Named as dean and professor of the School of Business Administration with Tulane University; also served as a visiting professor at INSEAD and Stanford University during the summers
1968-1971 and 1973-1975	Named dean and professor of the School of Business Administration with Southern Methodist University (SMU) in Dallas, Texas
1971-1973	Took leave from SMU when appointed chair of the U.S. Price Commission and successfully reduced inflation rate from five to two percent during his 15 month tenure
1973	Honored as Wharton's Man of the Year by the Wharton School at the University of Pennsylvania
1974	Published *Confessions of a Price Controller* with Louis Neeb
1975	Incorporated APC (the American Productivity Center) as a non-profit and created concept for an Executive Renewal Center
1975-present	Served as Founder, CEO, President, Chairman and Executive Chairman for APC—later known as APQC
1975-1977	Resigned SMU and began to raise $15 million of corporate support to launch APC
1975-1990	Served on the board of directors for eleven corporations for three decades
1977	Moved to Houston to establish APC and worked with Tom Fatjo to launch The Houstonian Hotel, Club & Spa
1978-1981	Named to Consultant Panel for Comptroller General of the United States
1980	Dedicated and opened APC headquarters building on grounds of The Houstonian Hotel, Club & Spa campus, also opened that year

1980	Named to President Carter's Commission for a National Agenda for the 80s
1981	Led first international benchmarking trip to Japan for White House Cabinet members, Congressional members, business executives and academics
1982	Named to President Reagan's National Productivity Advisory Committee
1982	Co-chaired first White House Conference on Productivity, hailed as the first "computer conference" with 175 business executives
1985-1988	Developed concept, criteria, funds and ultimately secured Congressional approval for the Malcolm Baldrige National Quality Award
1988	Changed the name of APC to become APQC (the American Productivity & Quality Center)
1988	Published *American Business: A Two-Minute Warning* with Carla O'Dell
1989	Held the first Baldrige Quest for Excellence conference with NIST for over 1000 attendees
1990	Lauded by *Business Week* which said "Few, if any, individual Americans have done more during the past 20 years to shape the country's economic future for the better."
1992	Launched APQC's International Benchmarking Clearinghouse service
1992	Developed APQC's Process Classification Framework® taxonomy, the most accessed file with more than 300,000 downloads since online tracking
1994	Held healthcare productivity conference in Houston with over 1000 attendees
1995	Held first knowledge management industry conference in Houston with over 500 attendees (20th anniversary conference in 2015)
1996	Conducted APQC's first research in the education sector

1998	Published *If Only We Knew What We Know* with Carla O'Dell
2000	Honored as one of 10 Most Admired Knowledge Leaders in the World by Teleos
2002	APQC honored as one of the 100 Companies That Matter in Knowledge Management by *KMWorld* magazine (and also honored in 2011, 2013 and 2014)
2003	Honored with Distinguished Service Medal from ASQ
2003	APQC honored with North American MAKE award for Most Admired Knowledge Enterprise (and also honored in 2004 and 2007-2013)
2003	Launched the APQC Knowledge Base, an online member portal of research and content
2003	Completed seven continent quest with Antarctica trip
2004	Launched APQC's Open Standards Benchmarking® database and service, noted as the world's largest with 17,000 survey submissions
2006	Honored with the C. Jackson Grayson Endowed Faculty Innovation Award and an Endowed Scholarship in Entrepreneurial Studies for MBAs by the Cox School of Business at SMU, a gift from Bobby Lyle
2008	Created the C. Jackson Grayson Distinguished Quality Pioneer Medal
2008	APQC honored with Global MAKE award for Most Admired Knowledge Enterprise (and also honored in 2011)
2009	Launched APQC's North Star Education Initiative
2011	*The New Edge in Knowledge: How Knowledge Management is Changing the Way We Do Business* by Carla O'Dell and Cindy Hubert is published
2011	APQC held first process conference in Houston
2011	APQC honored with Global MAKE Hall of Fame award
2012	APQC honored with Americas MAKE Hall of Fame award

2012	APQC honored as one of Houston's Top Workplaces by the *Houston Chronicle* (and also honored in 2013)
2013	APQC's Education Initiative published Grayson's *Transforming Education* report
2013	APQC introduced self-service benchmarking portal as a member benefit
2013	Grayson celebrated 90th birthday with a skydive
2014	APQC served more than 425 member organizations (550 counting subsidiary entities) from 48 countries
2014	Over 110 school districts have joined APQC's North Star Project to improve their processes
2014	Grayson biography *Freedom to Dream, Courage to Act* is published